Discourse dynamics

In this exciting new text Ian Parker provides one of the clearest and most systematic introductions to discourse research and essential theoretical debates in the area. It is one of the few texts to defend a realist position, discuss accounts of postmodernity and set out criteria for the identification of discourses.

Discourse Dynamics is addressed to both undergraduate students in psychology, and postgraduates and researchers new to discourse theory. It is essential reading to anyone interested in project research and an understanding of the issues involved in discourse analysis. The book will also be of use to students other than those studying psychology. It addresses the concerns of all those looking at qualitative textual research in the human sciences.

Ian Parker is a Lecturer in Social and Abnormal Psychology at Manchester Polytechnic. His other works include *The Crisis in Modern Social Psychology, and How to End it* (1989) and *Deconstructing Social Psychology* (1990) of which he was the co-editor.

Discourse dynamics

Critical analysis for social and
individual psychology

Ian Parker

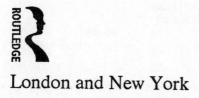

London and New York

First published in 1992
by Routledge
11 New Fetter Lane, London EC4P 4EE

Simultaneously published in the USA and Canada
by Routledge
a division of Routledge, Chapman and Hall, Inc.
29 West 35th Street, New York, NY 10001

Typeset from the author's wordprocessing disks by
NWL Editorial Services, Langport, Somerset

Printed and bound in Great Britain by
Biddles Ltd, Guildford and King's Lynn

British Library Cataloguing in Publication Data
Parker, Ian 1956–
  Discourse dynamics.
  1. Psycholinguistics
  I. Title
  401.9

Library of Congress Cataloging in Publication Data
Parker, Ian, 1956–
  Discourse dynamics/Ian Parker.
    p. cm.
  Includes bibliographical references and index.
  1. Discourse analysis – Psychological aspects. I. Title.
  P302.8.P37 1992   90–28866
  401'.41 – dc20   CIP

ISBN 0–415–05017–0
       0–415–05018–9 (pbk)

For Ben and Adam Beechey

Contents

Acknowledgements

The following people read versions of the chapters, and their comments and encouragement, even when they disagreed with what they saw, were important. Thanks – Erica Burman, Antony Easthope, Derek Edwards, Ros Gill, Adam James, John Kirkwood, Deborah Marks, Jonathan Potter, John Shotter, Robert Towers, Valerie Walkerdine, Heather Walton, Margaret Wetherell, Sue Widdicombe and Steve Woolgar.

Acknowledgements

Introduction

> It should be obvious, except perhaps to a *Guardian* reader, that ...
> the escaped Broadmoor killer, will be more dangerous to the
> public, rather than less, as result of having studied sociology at the
> Open University.
>
> (Worsthorne, 1983: 228)

You take your first step into discourse research as you take your first
step away from language. It is this paradox that makes the issues
covered in this book curious, useful, dangerous and liberating.

Language is so structured to mirror power relations that often we
can see no other ways of being, and it structures ideology so that it is
difficult to speak both in and against it. Outside psychology, studies
of language from a wide range of disciplines have shown how, for
example, gender is constructed and women are silenced (Spender,
1981), how colonialist visions of those outside the white West are
elaborated in language as 'other' (Said, 1978), and how notions of
class, knowledge and stupidity are connected in the ways we speak
(Andersen, 1988). Radical psychologists can draw on this work, and
do not need to call themselves 'discourse analysts' to do so. In fact, it
is better to start with a wish to deconstruct power and ideology and
then look at how a study of discourse dynamics could help. You have
to be, in some senses, outside psychology to do that. Inside psychology, the emergence of a discourse framework starts with the 'turn to
language'.

There are many strands to the turn to language in the discipline.
One of the influential forces here has been the group of writers who
participated in, and exacerbated, the 'crisis' in the late 1960s and early
1970s. The self-styled 'new paradigm' psychologists – a group which
includes Ken Gergen (1973, 1982), Rom Harré (1979, 1983) and

John Shotter (1975, 1984) – drew attention to the importance of meaning and the accounts people gave of their actions. These writers selectively imported ideas from microsociology – ethnomethodology, for example (Garfinkel, 1967) – and analytic philosophy – such as speech act theory (Austin, 1962). The new paradigm critiques of traditional laboratory-experimental social psychology are still relevant to contemporary debates about the role of (spoken or written) accounts as well as appropriate methods to study language, and they provide the context for the recent interest in discourse research.

Discourse analysis radicalizes the turn to language, but must also attempt to survive in a still powerful traditional climate of positivism in the discipline, the belief that an accumulation of little bits of 'objective' data about 'real' facts is the right way for a science of mental life to go on. This tradition has been divided, in social psychology, until the end of the 1980s, between those stubbornly clinging to orthodox, usually laughably trivial laboratory-experimental studies of individual behaviour and (more markedly in Europe than in America) those producing ostensibly more radical intergroup field studies. Across this, orthogonally as it were, the waves of research in attribution theory (with a massive influence), social cognition (with a sizeable following), social representations (less so) and now discourse analysis (increasingly) have swept across the discipline. It is discourse analysis that has caused most damage to the pretended internal coherence of social psychology. Developments in the study of language have also had some impact on other areas of psychology, leading to challenges to traditional personality theory and developmental psychology, and even to cognitive psychology (e.g., Harré et al., 1985; Costall and Still, 1987).

However, the crisis in psychology which has made discourse analysis possible was a pale reflection of debates over structures of meaning outside, debates which were to give issue to post-structuralism (Parker, 1989a). By post-structuralism I mean the set of writings on language, discourse and texts produced by a number of French cultural analysts, historians and philosophers in the 1960s, 1970s and 1980s, a group which includes Roland Barthes (1973, 1977), Jacques Derrida (1976, 1983), Michel Foucault (1977, 1980, 1981) and Jean-François Lyotard (1984). I will be drawing selectively and cautiously on work from this tradition to connect an analysis of discourse with studies of power and ideology in the course of this book.

My use and elaboration of ideas from discourse analysis is also highly selective. There is a rich source of research (e.g., van Dijk, 1985), which has yet to be tapped by psychology, which explores the links between fine-grained linguistic analysis and ideology. I focus on the role of repertoires, *discourses*, in the reproduction and transformation of meaning. Discourses both facilitate and limit, enable and constrain what can be said (by whom, where, when). I will be addressing debates in psychology over the role of discourse that have been brought to the fore by *Discourse and Social Psychology* (Potter and Wetherell, 1987), *Ideological Dilemmas* (Billig *et al.*, 1988) and *Subjectivity and Method in Psychology* (Hollway, 1989).

I take up definitions of discourse and the issue of realism in Part I. In Part II I focus on cultural changes and the notion of reflexivity, with an assessment of the advantages and disadvantages of this 'solution' to the powers of discourse in the turn to 'postmodern' psychology. I turn to look at models of the individual entailed by discourse approaches, and outline two alternatives (ecological and psychodynamic) to the now dominant cognitivist framework in psychology in Part III. The book ends with a fairly exhaustive research guide to the study of discourse in social and individual psychology.

There are intimate links between knowledge and power, and, in this culture, between discourses of knowledge and ideology. This book is not about 'method', though it may help develop some expertise in the analysis of discourse and I suggest some steps along the way. The book is about the dynamics that run through the operation of different discourses, the cultural dynamics that affect the way we use discourse and the subjective dynamics which tear at our sense of self as discourses use us.

Part I

Discourses

Discourse analysis already has a history in psychology, and I set the scene for an analysis of discourse dynamics in this first part of the book. In the first chapter I work through the consequences of a definition of discourses as sets of statements which constitute an object. I elaborate a set of criteria for defining what a discourse is. I run through seven necessary criteria and then three additional points to do with institutions, power and ideology. Through these criteria I use post-structuralist work on discourse to show how the study of language must attend to tensions and contradictions which express political matters. Without these three supplementary points, an analysis of discourse could become just another method, just an academic exercise, and then just as pointless as other frameworks psychologists use to describe action and experience.

I cannot pretend that a focus on institutions, power and ideology is not a moral/political matter (and perhaps it is only that), and the following chapters in this book rest on the assumption that amoral/apolitical psychology is worse than useless. Each theoretical resource used by discourse analysts in psychology (whether it be sociology of scientific knowledge, microsociology, analytic philosophy, rhetoric, semiology or post-structuralism) can all too easily draw us into versions of linguistic relativism, idealism. A focus on the structures of language at the expense of an analysis of material coercion is one that discourse analysts feel differently, and ambivalently, about. Chapter 2 takes this issue seriously, and outlines a realist view of language and the material resources which make discourse possible. The study of the dynamics which structure texts has to be located in an account of the ways discourses reproduce and transform the material world.

Chapter 1

Discovering discourses, tackling texts

A means of indicating the transition from a sign to a sign is offered by quotation marks. Thus 'California' is a sign that denotes California; 'California' is written with ten letters, whereas California grows oranges. The transition may be further repeated. Thus "California" is the name of a sign, namely of 'California', but is not the name of California. In writing quotes we have to watch that the sign combination occurring in our sentence is always one level higher than the object to which it refers. Thus "California" is written with one pair of quotes, and 'California' is written without quotes. It would be difficult to add quotes to California; we then would have to construct huge quotes and put those of the left end into the Pacific Ocean, and those of the right end into Nevada.

(Reichenbach 1947: 68)

What is a 'discourse'? This chapter is concerned with the task of defining discourses. I will draw attention to some of the descriptions of discourse outside psychology, and then set out some criteria for identifying discourses. My main focus will be on the practical problems which confront a researcher attempting to carry out a discourse analysis. However, each practical problem raises broader issues about the nature of language, discourse and texts. I will also argue, towards the end of the chapter, that discourse analytic research should go beyond seven necessary criteria for the identification of discourses, and consider the role of institutions, power and ideology.

Discourse research strikes a critical distance from language, and one useful aspect of the approach is the reflexivity urged upon a researcher, and reader. When discourse analysts read texts they are continually putting what they read into quotation marks: 'Why was this said, and not that? Why these words, and where do the connotations of the words fit with different ways of talking about the world?' I want to argue, however, that this reflexivity needs to be grounded if it is to have progressive effects, and that work in the post-structuralist tradition can ground discourse and reflection historically in a useful way. In addition, the study of discourses carried out by Foucault and his followers has implications for how we describe the emergence of academic psychology and the 'psy-complex' in Western culture, and for how we understand the discipline and its objects today (Rose, 1985, 1989).

Foucault (1971), for example, described how a discourse which was about 'madness' as a medical category came into being, and the ways in which a medical discourse emerged alongside related ways of speaking about individual 'pathology' which involved the categorisation of a section of the population. Debates over rationality and responsibility in the nineteenth century were informed by such discourses. In another study Foucault (1975) and co-workers collected legal papers and accounts given of a murder at that time, and showed how discourses of individual reason and 'madness' framed the possible explanations that could be given of the event. Foucault (1977, 1981) also connected the development of discourses which describe and prescribe forms of rationality, responsibility and pathology with discipline, surveillance and power. These discourses informed legal practice, and they helped constitute contemporary psychology. Discourses about the person that we employ today, then, have a history.

It is also possible for discourses about the nature of mental processes, and to whom one attributes them, to fall into disuse. At the beginning of the century, for example, at the very moment when 'cross-cultural' psychology was busily demarcating certain human 'races' as not fully mentally developed, there was an area of research devoted to plant psychology (Crellin, 1989). The attribution of mental states was framed by discourses pertaining to plants as almost sentient beings. In contrast, the dominant psychology we have today is informed by particular conceptions of rationality, discourses in which one attributes to individual human beings internal mental states which, we suppose, direct behaviour (Costall and Still, 1987).

A number of issues arise from the history of discourse. Discourses do not simply describe the social world, but categorise it, they bring phenomena into sight. A strong form of the argument would be that discourses allow us to see things that are not 'really' there, and that once an object has been elaborated in a discourse it is difficult *not* to refer to it as if it were real. Discourses provide frameworks for debating the value of one way of talking about reality over other ways. Types of person are also being referred to as the objects of the discourses. When we look at discourses in their historical context, it becomes clear that they are quite coherent, and that as they are elaborated by academics and in everyday life they become more carefully systematised. Discourse analysis *deliberately* systematises different ways of talking so we can understand them better. A study of discourse dynamics takes off from this to look at the tensions within discourses and the way they reproduce and transform the world.

A good working definition of a discourse should be that it is *a system of statements which constructs an object*. However, this definition needs to be supported by a number of conditions. In the main section of this chapter, then, I will set out seven criteria, the system of statements that should be used to identify *our* object, to enable us to engage with, and in, discourse analysis. Potter and Wetherell's (1987) account of the 'method', their 'ten stages in the analysis of discourse', is useful, but sometimes bewilders new researchers as it dawns on them that each step rests on a bedrock of 'intuition' and 'presentation'. At points the reader is told, quite rightly, that discourse analysis is like riding a bike, is warned that the stages are not sequential, and advised that 'there is no analytic method' (Potter and Wetherell, 1987: 169). Billig *et al.*'s (1988) suggestions that a researcher needs to look for 'implicit themes' is also right, but can also lead to worries on the part of someone new to the area that they may not be picking up the themes that matter. Similarly, when Hollway (1989) draws on her own intuitive feel for what is going on in discourse, how the accounts of her interviewees resonate with her own experience, she produces fascinating and plausible analyses. But how could we do this too? I do not want to suggest that the criteria presented here constitute a method, that they should necessarily be employed sequentially, but that they will help to clear up some of the confusions that have followed the incorporation of discourse ideas into psychology.

SEVEN CRITERIA FOR DISTINGUISHING DISCOURSES

These seven criteria deal with different levels of discourse analysis. There is a degree of conceptual work that needs to go into the analysis before the material is touched, and then, as the analysis proceeds, it is necessary to step back a number of times to make sense of the statements that have been picked out. Each criterion raises questions about the theoretical framework the researcher is using. Along the way I will mark some 'steps' in an analysis of discourse dynamics (and you will have to imagine quotation marks around the word 'steps' from now on).

1) A discourse is realised in texts

First, though, where do we find discourses? It would be misleading to say that we ever find discourses as such. We actually find pieces of discourse. I want to open up the field of meanings to which discourse analysis could be applied beyond spoken interaction and written forms by saying that we find discourses at work in *texts*. Texts are delimited tissues of meaning reproduced in *any* form that can be given an interpretative gloss.

Take two examples: (i) I was given a small Liquid Crystal Display electronic game for Christmas. The buttons on the left and right move a male figure at the bottom of the screen from side to side. The figure is waving a crucifix at the ghosts descending from the top of the screen to their graves. As each ghost is prevented from landing and is despatched to the flames at the right-hand side I get awarded ten points (and the penalty for letting each spirit through is a lost life). This is a text. A Christian discourse inhabits this text, and it is the translation of this text into a written and spoken form that renders that discourse 'visible' or, more accurately, in which the category 'discourse' becomes appropriate; (ii) as I work through this chapter a second time a melody comes wafting up the stairs. The unmarried couple I share a house with are playing host to her parents who have come to cosset the new baby. Grand-dad has got his hands on the electric organ and is quietly finding his way round the keyboard. The tune is uncertain snatches of 'Here comes the bride'. A little narrative of heterosexual bonding within familial discourse inhabits this melody as the text.

It is useful, as a first step, to consider all tissues of meaning as texts and to specify which texts will be studied. All of the world, when it has become a world understood by us and so given meaning by us, can be described as being textual. Once the process of interpretation and reflection has been started, we can adopt the post-structuralist maxim '*[t]here is nothing outside of the text*' (Derrida, 1976: 158). This does not necessarily commit us to a particular position on the nature of reality, textual or otherwise. I deal with that issue in the next chapter. I am merely drawing attention to the effects of describing, for research purposes, the world in this way. Speech, writing, non-verbal behaviour, Braille, Morse code, semaphore, runes, advertisements, fashion systems, stained glass, architecture, tarot cards and bus tickets are all forms of text. In some cases we could imagine an 'author' lying behind the text as source and arbiter of a true meaning. But the lessons to draw from this list are, first, that, as Barthes (1977) argued, there need not be an author, and, second, that once we start to describe what texts mean we are elaborating meanings that go beyond individual intentions, discourses that are transindividual. The second step in a discourse analysis, then, should be a process of exploring the connotations, allusions and implications which the texts evoke. A helpful guide to this exercise in cultural anthropology is Barthes' (1973) work on modern 'myth'.

Sometimes different discourses are available to different audiences. The distinction between the inside and outside of psychology is a good case example. On the one hand, the ψ sign gives a text a meaning for those of us inside psychology. The discourses which inhabit a text containing that sign will often be discourses coherent to psychologists. On the other hand, an image of Freud's face gives a text a meaning for those outside the discipline. The discourses which give that sign meaning, and it often means 'psychology' for outsiders, would not be accepted by many psychologists. It is right, then, to adopt the formulation that discourses are 'linguistic sets of a higher order than the sentence (while often reducible to a sentence) and *carried out* or *actualized* in or by means of texts' (Marin, 1983: 162). Discourse analysis, then, involves two preliminary steps:

1 Treating our objects of study as texts which are described, put into words; and

2 Exploring connotations through some sort of free association, which is best done with other people.

2) A discourse is about objects

'Analysis' necessarily entails some degree of objectification, and in studies of discourse there are at least two layers of objectification. The first is the layer of 'reality' that the discourse refers to. It is a commonplace in the sociology of knowledge (e.g., Berger and Luckmann, 1971) that language brings into being phenomena, and that the reference to something, the simple use of a noun, comes to give that object a reality. Discourses are the sets of meanings which constitute objects, and a discourse, then, is indeed a 'representational practice' (Woolgar, 1988a: 93). The representation of the object occurs as previous uses of the discourse and other related discourses are alluded to, and the object *as defined in the discourses* is referred to. Some local councils have had to close off sewer entrances to stop young children from going down to look for ninja turtles. The turtle discourse constitutes these beings as objects for children, and when the children refer to turtles they are referring to the objects of the discourse. They think, as most of us do when we talk about things, that they are talking about real objects in the world. Discourses are, according to one post-structuralist writer, 'practices that system- atically form the objects of which they speak' (Foucault, 1972: 49).

Discourse constructs 'representations' of the world which have a reality almost as coercive as gravity, and, like gravity, we know of the objects through their effects. Take, for example, descriptions of medi- eval Anglo-Saxon sorcery in which the world is full of spirits and physical illness is attributed to the shots fired by elves (Bates, 1983). What we now can describe as 'discourses' created and reproduced spirits and elves. Then, they were real in the way that atoms and electrons are real today. Many of the objects that discourse refers to do not exist in a realm outside discourse. There are fuzzy borders between the set of things we know exist outside discourse and the things which may have a reality only within it. The first layer of reality, then, is the reality of the objects of the discourse, the things the discourse refers to.

The second layer of reality, of objectification that a discourse sometimes refers to is that of the discourse itself. One example is a badge given away at the Commonwealth Institute in London in 1988 with 'Dialogue on Diarrhoea' printed around the top. It says 'international newsletter' around the bottom, and these phrases frame a picture of a woman feeding an infant with a spoon. There were also huge posters around the cafeteria with the same message blazoned across them. At the first level of meaning, we have the object 'diarrhoea', and the badge is a text which reproduces the object in particular ways: (i) we know that 'diarrhoea' is, among other things, a medical description, and so we can identify a medical discourse; (ii) we assume that the woman feeding the infant is the mother, and so a familialist discourse also touches the text; and (iii) we understand the image and message as located in an appeal, located in a discourse of charity. The *second* layer of reality, then, is that of the 'dialogue', and here there is a reflection in the text on a discourse, and the text says that there is another 'object' which is the set of statements about diarrhoea. A discourse is about objects, and discourse analysis is about *discourses* as objects. This criterion, then, takes us into a third and a fourth step of analysis:

3 Asking what objects are referred to, and describing them (turtles, diseases, ghosts etc.); and
4 Talking about the talk as if it were an object, a discourse.

3) A discourse contains subjects

The object that a discourse refers to may have an independent reality outside discourse, but is given *another* reality by discourse. An example of such an object is the subject who speaks, writes, hears or reads the texts discourses inhabit. I will stick with this rather abstract and dehumanising jargon a moment longer and say that a subject, a sense of self, is a location constructed within the expressive sphere which finds its voice through the cluster of attributes and responsibilities assigned to it as a variety of object. (Here, you may find it helpful to think of Harré's (1979) distinction between the 'expressive' sphere in which meanings and selves are presented and contested and the 'practical' order of society in which the physical world is organised and worked to sustain life.) A discourse makes available a space for particular types of self to step in. It addresses us in a particular way. When we discourse analyse a text, we need to ask in what ways, as Althusser (1971) put it when he was talking about the appeal of ideology, the discourse is hailing us, shouting 'hey you there' and making us listen as a certain type of person.

It has been said that discourses are 'ways of perceiving and articulating relationships' (Banton *et al.*, 1985: 16). This is right, but it is more than that, for we cannot avoid the perceptions of ourselves and others that discourses invite. There are two ways in which this works, and discourse analysis both attends to and intensifies each of these. First, there is the relation between the addressor (which we should think of here as being the text rather than the author who may have originated it) and the addressee. When a badge says 'Dialogue on Diarrhoea', who is it addressing? To put it crudely, and to employ an old social-psychological discourse, what 'role' are we having to adopt to hear this message? (i) a medical discourse could draw us in as a carer, but merely to supplement the work of those who are medically qualified; (ii) the familialist discourse draws us in as protector (with different subject effects depending on the gender position we have in other discourses); and (iii) the charity discourse draws us in as benefactor, 'millionaire philanthropist in stately Wayne Manor' say, and the 'dialogue' is about listening, understanding and giving.

The second way in which we are positioned as a subject in discourse flows from that last point about what we are expected to do when addressed. What rights do we have to speak in a discourse? The medical discourse, for example, is one in which we adopt the position of nonmedic, and, while we may use a medical vocabulary in some situations, there are others in which it is inappropriate. At the doctor's surgery, for example, the translation of the deliberately prosaic and everyday language *we* use into medical terminology is *their* task. We know we are the patient in this discourse. We are also positioned in a relation of power when we are placed in relation to the discourse itself. A (pseudo-)scientific discourse such as psychology, for example, is one in which rights and powers to speak are clearly signalled by the amount of knowledge held, and the desire to be a scientist may be provoked when we hear or use that discourse. We may also resist it, but we have to take a position. This brings us to fifth and sixth steps in analysis:

5 Specifying what types of person are talked about in this discourse, some of which may already have been identified as objects (turtles, doctors, mothers, benefactors, etc.); and
6 Speculating about what they can say in the discourse, what you could say if you identified with them (what rights to speak in that way of speaking).

4) A discourse is a coherent system of meanings

The metaphors, analogies and pictures discourses paint of a reality can be distilled into statements about that reality. It is only then that it becomes possible to say that a discourse is 'any regulated system of statements' (Henriques *et al.*, 1984: 105). This notion of discourse explicitly draws on Foucault's work. The statements in a discourse can be grouped, and given a certain coherence, insofar as they refer to the same topic. We have to employ culturally available understanding as to what constitutes a topic or theme, here making a virtue of the fact that there are different competing cultures which will give different slants on the discourse, ranging from those whom the discourse benefits (and who may not even want to recognise it as a discourse) to those whom it oppresses (who are already angry about that way of talking about things and categorising people in that way). This is not to say that the set of statements is ever watertight. I will return to the role of contradictions within particular discourses under the next heading.

There is a similarity here between this aspect of a definition of discourses and the way 'interpretative repertoires' are defined in *Discourse and Social Psychology*. It is worth building on the idea that we are indeed looking for 'recurrently used systems of terms used for characterizing and evaluating actions, events and other phenomena . . . a limited range of terms used in particular stylistic and grammatical constructions . . . [often] . . . organized around specific metaphors and figures of speech' (Potter and Wetherell, 1987: 149). We should be cautious, though, about three aspects of this label 'interpretative repertoire': (i) to talk about 'grammatical constructions' is inappropriate and risks getting bogged down in formalism at the expense of content; (ii) the assertion that there is a 'limited range of terms' feeds the positivist fantasy for an ultimate complete picture of a particular system, a totality of meanings; and (iii) the term 'repertoire' has uncomfortable resonances with behaviourism, especially when we are invited to look for systems of terms which are 'recurrently used'. There is a case for adopting the term repertoire to catch the almost physical positioning of a person as they turn in a text along the lines of pre-existing representations of the world, perhaps in the way that Barthes (1990) talks about a 'figure' moving through space (Margaret Wetherell, pers. comm.), but it is surely better to label sets of metaphors and statements we find as *'discourses'*. (This is the term I use throughout this book.)

To return to the problem of how to recognise one discourse when faced with a mass of text, how do we employ this notion of coherence? Take the example of Dan Quayle, American vice-president, speaking at a Thanksgiving festival:

I suppose three important things certainly come to my mind that we want to say thank you [for]. The first would be our family. Your family, my family – which is composed of an immediate family of a wife and three children, a larger family with grandparents and aunts and uncles. We all have our family, whichever that may be. . . . The family . . . which goes back to the nucleus of civilisation. And the very beginnings of civilisation, the very beginnings of this country, goes back to the family. And time and time again, I'm often reminded, especially in this presidential campaign, of the importance of the family, and what a family means to this country. And so when you pay thanks I suppose the first thing that would come to mind would be to thank the Lord for the family.

(*Guardian*, 8 November 1988)

Quayle attempts to define the 'family', but what I want to draw attention to here is the way we have to bring our own sense of what 'the family' is to this text in order to make it coherent, to string these repeated references to 'the family' together so we recognise it as a discourse with an object (the family) and with subjects (mothers, fathers, children). In this case we are able to do this because there is such a strong 'familialist discourse' in our culture: 'society has been familiarized' (Barrett and McIntosh, 1982: 31). But we also have to bring a knowledge of discourses from outside, our awareness in this case that this is not the only way of talking about relationships, to bear on any example or fragment of discourse for it to become part of a coherent system in our analysis. A seventh and an eighth step can be taken here, in which we are:

7 Mapping a picture of the world this discourse presents (running in accordance with God's plans, through the operation of discourses, at the mercy of hidden conspiracies, etc.); and

8 Working out how a text using this discourse would deal with objections to the terminology (sinful doubt, crude out-of-date materialism, receipt of Moscow gold, etc.).

5) A discourse refers to other discourses

Post-structuralists contend that thought is bound up with language, and that reflexivity is continually captured, and distorted, by language (Descombes, 1980). If they are right then reflexivity itself should be understood to be merely the employment of available discourses. At the very least, to take a weaker line on this, the *articulation* of our reflections on discourse must require the use of discourses. A critical reflection on a discourse will often involve the use of other discourses. Talking about the inability to use certain discourses in terms of 'repression', for example, could be seen as the use of psycho-analytic discourse rather than the discovery of a profound truth. Foucault's (1981) devastating historical critique of psychoanalysis starts from this point, and goes on to describe the way people using this discourse are compelled to use it more and more in a spiral of (what they think is) reflexivity and deeper truth.

Discourses embed, entail and presuppose other discourses to the extent that the contradictions *within* a discourse open up questions about what other discourses are at work. For example, my children wanted to see the Mona Lisa when we went to Paris because it was painted by Leonardo, who is one of the ninja turtles. The turtle discourse which constituted the painting as one type of object can be understood as 'just' a discourse by a competing discourse of artistic genius, one which captures most of the Louvre visitors in its vice-like grip as they admire the picture.

It is in this sense that it is right to argue that '[t]he systematic character of a discourse includes its systematic articulation with other discourses. In practice, discourses delimit what can be said, whilst providing the spaces – the concepts, metaphors, models, analogies – for making new statements within any specific discourse' (Henriques *et al.* 1984: 105–6). This point raises, in turn, two further issues. First, metaphors and analogies are always available from other discourses, and the space this gives a speaker to find a voice from another discourse, and even within a discourse they oppose, is theoretically limitless. (It is not limitless in practice. I will take up this point when I discuss the role of institutions, power and ideology in the next section of this chapter.)

Second, analysis is facilitated by identifying contradictions between different ways of describing something. The examples I have referred to so far include familialist discourse and Christian discourse, and these interrelate in various paradoxical ways with racist discourses. It is possible to imagine ways in which each of these can contradict the others. The metaphors of family used to describe the human race used alongside the currently popular liberal-humanist discourse could characterise Christian doctrine and racism as coterminous and equally dangerous (Barthes, 1973). Alternatively, some versions of liberation theology include conceptions of community which are suspicous of the nuclear family and are committed to anti-racism (Löwy, 1988). Then again, racist discourses which appeal to mysticism take forms hostile to the modern family and liberal Christianity (Trotsky, 1933).

Now, I am *not* intending to imply that each of these discourses is discrete in practice. You may have to stretch your imagination to accept some of the combinations I suggested. At the moment, it could be argued that the discourses draw metaphors and institutional support from each other, and the process of distinguishing them is purely conceptual. Well, this is precisely the point, for we need to understand the *interrelationship*, the interrelationship between *different* discourses in an analysis. In the ninth and tenth steps of an analysis, then, we can start:

9 Setting contrasting ways of speaking, discourses, against each other and looking at the different objects they constitute (brains, souls, epiphenomena, etc.); and

10 Identifying points where they overlap, where they constitute what look like the 'same' objects in different ways (secretions of neural matter, immortal spiritual essences, rhetorical devices, etc.).

6) A discourse reflects on its own way of speaking

Not every text contains a reflection on the terms chosen, and not every speaker is self-conscious about the language they use. However, a condition which applies to each discourse taken as a whole is that it is possible to find instances where the terms chosen are commented upon. At these points, the discourse itself folds around and reflects on its own way of speaking. The devices employed to bring about this reflection range from the uneasy phrase 'for the want of a better word' through disingenuous denials of a position being advocated – 'don't get me wrong' – to full-blown agonising as to the moral implications of a world-view.

This raises the issue of 'intuition' in the research, for the analyst needs to be able to step into the discourse at points to get a sense of what it feels like as a coherent whole. How are the contradictions in the discourse referred to, and how would another person or text employing this discourse refer to the contradictions within the discourse? When these questions are answered, other instances of a discourse can be identified, and it is important here not only to articulate instances of a discourse into a coherent pattern, but also to take it back where possible to the speaker, an interviewee perhaps, or to relate it to other texts.

A related point has been made by the authors of *Ideological Dilemmas*, that it is necessary to attend to different layers of meaning. Working on the assumption that assertions in a discourse also pose an opposing position, by virtue of the 'dilemmatic' nature of language and thought, they argue that we should attend to 'hidden meanings': 'discourse can contain its own negations, and these are part of its implicit, rather than explicit meaning' (Billig *et al.*, 1988: 23). They suggest that we should engage in hermeneutics to recover these meanings. A hermeneutic style of inquiry is being used at points in discourse analysis, but it is a type of hermeneutics which does not attempt to trace the meanings to an author (e.g., Ricoeur, 1971). What we can take from this is the idea that analysis should bring in other readers and listeners, and use their understanding of a discourse to bring out the implicit meanings, the views which are rarely voiced but which are part of that way of talking about things.

For the discourse analyst, the reflexivity of a discourse is found at points which will probably be found in other texts when it folds around to note its own nature as an argument or theory. Finding these points can be useful as a marker that the discourse analyst is actually picking up a discrete discourse. We can also think of this part of the research as proceeding through an eleventh and a twelfth step in which we are:

11 Referring to other texts to elaborate the discourse as it occurs, perhaps implicitly, and addresses different audiences (in children's books, advertisements, jokes, etc.) and;
12 Reflecting on the term used to describe the discourse, a matter which involves moral/political choices on the part of the analyst (describing discourses about 'race' as 'racist' discourses, for example).

7) A discourse is historically located

Discourses are not static. I have already pointed to the relationship between different discourses, and the ways in which discourses change and develop different layers and connections to other discourses through the process of reflection. When we think about discourses as consisting of a system of statements, it could appear as if an appeal is being made to the 'synchronic' dimension of language which inspired structural linguistics (Saussure, 1974). However, just as post-structuralism moved beyond the distinction between a system (the 'synchronic') and the development of individual terms (the 'diachronic'), so discourse analysis cannot take place without locating its object in time. Discourses are located in time, in history, for the objects they refer to are objects constituted in the past by the discourse or related discourses. A discourse refers to past references to those objects.

For discourse analysts, the structure and force of particular discourses can only be described by showing other instances of that discourse, and explaining how it arose. The familialist discourse, for example, includes a history of the family and the way that history is reinterpreted to legitimate the Western nuclear family form. The way the metaphors of family are used are not only to describe other forms of life, but also often to reinforce the notion of the family as natural, as going back to the beginnings of civilisation. When we analyse the discourse of the family, we are disconnecting ourselves from that history. Similarly, discourse analysis of religion and racism switches back and forward from the elaboration of coherent systems of statements out of the texts it studies to look at what those discourses meant as they emerged, and so what the present allusions actually 'refer' to.

It then becomes possible to use our knowledge of the historical weight of racist and religious discourses, say, to understand occasions when they combine. One reflection on the importance of language comes together with these themes in a statement made in 1986 by a supporter of a campaign in Southern California against the use of Spanish as a second language in the state. It ran: 'If English was good enough for Jesus Christ, it's good enough for me.' Of course, a reading of this phrase needs not only an understanding of what discourses there are and how they arose. It also calls for a study of the types of texts within which those discourses became dominant in the last fifty years or so. (My guess in this case would be that Hollywood films would be powerful texts in which these discourses fused and altered each other.) This prompts two further steps for the analyst in which she is:

13 Looking at how and where the discourses emerged; and
14 Describing how they have changed, and told a story, usually about how they refer to things which were always there to be discovered.

We have arrived, through these criteria and steps, at a sense of discourse as something dynamic and changing, but we need to go a little further to make the analysis politically useful.

THREE AUXILIARY CRITERIA

Although the seven criteria I have outlined are necessary and sufficient for marking out particular discourses, I want to draw attention to three more aspects of discourse that research *should* focus upon. The three further aspects of discourse are concerned with institutions, power and ideology. I will go through each in turn, and indicate why each is important and why these final three should be worked through in an analysis.

8) Discourses support institutions

The most interesting discourses are those which are implicated in some way with the structure of institutions. The medical discourse, for example, exists in a variety of texts – medical journals and books, research reports, lectures, General Medical Council decisions and popular medicine programmes, as well as the speech in every consultation with a doctor. In cases such as these, the employment of a discourse is also often a practice which reproduces the material basis of the institution. Feeling an abdomen, giving an injection or cutting a body are *discursive practices*. For Foucault (1972), discourses and practices should be treated as if they were the same thing, and it is true both that material practices are always invested with meaning (they have the status of a text) and that speaking or writing is a 'practice'. Foucault's (1977) work on discipline and power is concerned with the ways in which the physical organisation of space and bodies developed.

However, it is also possible, and more useful, to identify a distinction between physical order and meanings in his work, and it is helpful to hold onto a conceptual distinction between meanings, the expressive, and physical changes, the practical order (Harré, 1979). 'Discursive practices', then, would be those that reproduce institutions, among other things. An academic Discourse Group could operate as an institution, for example, if it could validate or prevent certain styles of discourse analysis. Happily, at the moment discourse analysts reproduce a discourse about discourse which operates in a contradictory way in relation to institutions. Radical analysts could start by:

15 Identifying institutions which are reinforced when this or that discourse is used; and
16 Identifying institutions that are attacked or subverted when this or that discourse appears.

9) Discourses reproduce power relations

We *should* talk about discourse and power in the same breath. Institutions, for example, are structured around and reproduce power relations. The giving and taking away of rights to speak in medical discourse and the powerlessness patients feel when in the grip of medical technology are examples of the intimate link between power and knowledge (Turner, 1987). A phenomenon that a discourse analysis which employed my three auxiliary criteria as well as the first seven outlined above could usefully explore is the way that when psychology in Britain becomes a 'Chartered' profession it will both be able to popularise the discourses which constitute its objects ('behaviours', 'cognitions' and suchlike) *and* be able to police the boundaries between its regime of truth and the others outside, the 'charlatans'. Psychology's increasing institutionalisation will, in this way, increase its *power* over both those outside and those inside it.

Foucault (1980) and his followers popularised the couplet 'power/knowledge', but the two terms are not the same thing. It is important to distinguish discourse from power. Discourses often do reproduce power relations, but this is a different claim from one which proposes that a criterion for recognising a discourse is that there is power. If this criterion were to be adopted, we would fall into the trap of saying that 'power is everywhere' and that, if power is everywhere, it would be both pointless to refer to it and politically fruitless to attack it (Poulantzas, 1978). There are three good reasons why we should not talk about discourse and power as *necessarily* entailing one another: (i) we would lose a sense of the relationship between power and resistance, lose the distinction between power as coercive and resistance as a refusal of dominant meanings; (ii) we would lose sight of the ways in which discourses that challenge power are often tangled in oppressive discourses, but are no less valuable to our understanding of relationships and possible future relationships for that; and (iii) it would be difficult, as researchers, to support the empowerment of those at the sharp end of dominant discourses and discursive practices. The further steps an analyst could take here include:

17 Looking at which categories of person gain and lose from the employment of the discourse; and
18 Looking at who would want to promote and who would want to dissolve the discourse.

10) Discourses have ideological effects

Lying behind each of the objections to confusing discourse and power, of course, is a political position. This has to be even more explicitly marked when we talk about ideology. One deleterious effect of the rise of discourse analysis has been that the category of ideology virtually disappeared. In part, this has been a result of Foucault's (1980) insistence that the term ideology presupposes truth, and that we should instead, speak of 'regimes of truth' in which one regime is no more correct than any other. It is right, I think, to say that discourse analysis need not necessarily be concerned with ideology, but it would be wrong to avoid it altogether. The use of the category of ideology has progressive political effects, and it is not necessary to buy the whole package of 'mystification' and 'false consciousness' that Foucauldians caricature (e.g., Henriques *et al.*, 1984). However, if we are to hold onto the term 'ideology', there are two theoretical traps we do need to avoid.

The first trap is to say that *all* discourses are ideological, and thus to follow in the steps of some sociologists who claim that 'ideology' is equivalent to a belief system (e.g., Bell, 1965). As with the category of power, this position sees ideology everywhere and makes the term redundant. It neatly folds into the discourse which claims that the ideas of those who resist existing power relations are as ideological as those who support them, and it has similar political effects. This relativism either evacuates politics of any meaning (other than leaving things as they are) or confines politics to the sphere of individual moral choice. Both these positions are ideological positions. The second danger is that we try and distinguish between discourses which are ideological and those which tell the truth. For those who want to defend the use of the category of ideology, this is the simpler and more attractive trap.

The mistake being made in both these cases is that ideology is being treated as a thing, or is being evaluated according to its content. We should see ideology, rather, as a description of *relationships* and *effects*, and the category should be employed to describe relationships at a particular place and historical period. It could be, for example, that Christian discourse functions in an ideological way when it buttresses racism as a dominant world-view. But it is also *possible* that such a discourse can be empowering, and that even claims that it is a 'subjugated knowledge', in Foucauldian jargon, could be well founded (Mudge, 1987). If discourse analysis is to be informed by descriptions of institutions, power and ideology, then the history of discourses becomes even more important. The final 'radical steps', then, would involve:

19 Showing how a discourse connects with other discourses which sanction oppression; and
20 Showing how the discourses allow dominant groups to tell their narratives about the past in order to justify the present, and prevent those who use subjugated discourses from making history.

The six supplementary steps cannot be taken without the elaboration of political motives, and I deal with such motives in the course of this book. That they are supplementary steps, and support auxiliary criteria, is evidence that discourse analysis could become just another psychological method, something which I think we should resist.

CONCLUSIONS AND REFLECTIONS

The three auxiliary criteria I have proposed, and in particular the final one concerned with ideology, prompt a question which is implicit in much of the discourse analysis literature, and which occurs routinely in discussions with those new to the area: 'how do we escape discourse?' If it is true that discourses frame the way we think about the objects they construct, and the way we are positioned as subjects, is there any way out? Well, one way out is to address the question instead of attempting to answer it. We need not answer the question. It is loaded against radical discourse analysts, and that is why it is continually thrown at us. Four points can be made to support the tactic of *not* answering the question.

First of all, attempts to *escape* discourse invite us to regress to exactly those conceptions of individual culpability for social practices that discourse analysis attempts to avoid. When we choose words that have connotations we think we did not intend, and which effectively reproduce a discourse we know is oppressive, this does not mean we have failed to follow the path of the good and true. Discourse analysis draws attention to language, and can help us reflect on what we do when we speak (or write), but the *reflexivity* advocated by some discourse analysts is not a solution. Reflexivity is necessary and has been employed to good effect in discourse analytic work, but it does not dissolve discourse.

A second related point is that we need to be cautious about what discourse analysis can accomplish. If we take the first seven criteria, then we shift the balance of the discipline from being, in Rorty's (1980) terms, a 'systematising' approach to an 'edifying' type of inquiry. We cannot escape systematising when we research into discourse. However, discourse analysis should bring about an understanding of the way things *were*, not the way things are. Another way of putting this is to say that when we strike a critical distance from a discourse we, in a sense, put it behind us, consign it to the past. If we adopt the three auxiliary criteria, we describe, educate and change the way discourse is used. Discourse analysis should become a variety of action research, in which the internal system of any discourse and its relation to others is challenged. It alters, and so permits different spaces for manoeuvre and resistance.

A third point connected with the previous two is that both reflexivity and discourse analysis are historically and culturally bound. This is not to say that people in other cultures do not reflect on what they do, but that reflexivity seen as a solution is specific to our time and place in Western culture. Similarly, this should not be taken to mean that it would be impossible to go and pick out discourses in other cultures. We now have specified an object which is discourse, and we could see it everywhere in the world where there is meaning. We have not 'discovered' it, but it is available for us as a topic, and we have to intervene in the contradictions it contains. Discourse analysis is both a symptom and part of the cure: the preoccupation with language in contemporary psychology is a symptom of an evasion of the material basis of oppression on the part of academics, but an attention to language can also facilitate a process of progressively politicising everyday life. Linked to the positive side of this process is the feminist claim that the personal is political (Rowbotham *et al.*, 1979). It is no accident that the 'turn-to-language' was paralleled, and then followed through most thoroughly with an attention to power outside psychology by feminist researchers (e.g., Spender, 1981; Stanley and Wise, 1983).

A fourth and final point relates to the politics of discourse analysis and to the importance of contradiction. Politics here is bound up with history, both in the sense that we have discourse now at this point in history (here we feel the weight of the past), and in the sense that politics and power are about the ability to push history in particular ways (there we construct a hope for the future). The difference between discourses is aggravated as one discourse is employed to supersede the other. When progress and change are notions built into contemporary political discourse, and things are changing so fast, it is hardly surprising that this dynamic should be reflected in our everyday experience of language. In political debate, the dynamics of resistance are of this discursive kind, and we have to have a sense of where discourses are coming from and where they are going to understand which are the progressive and which the reactionary ideas at different times and places. I deal with the issues raised by these third and fourth points in Part II of this book, for it is here that we need a sense of wider cultural dynamics.

At the beginning of this chapter I briefly described histories of 'psychology' in which attention was drawn to the ways rationality and responsibility have been located in the minds of individuals. Inside the discipline these burdens have been supplemented by a variety of cognitive paraphernalia, and this has been supported by, and in some cases necessitated, the operation of a variety of dubious discursive practices (Shotter, 1987). The advantage of discourse analysis is that it reframes the object, and individual's psychology, and allows us to treat it not as truth, but as one 'truth' held in place by language and power. Now the old question about whether our discipline is helpful or harmful seems to depend on our place in a contradiction between two views of truth, whether one takes the side of psychology or the side of discourse. It seems to. The point we need to bear in mind, though, is that in order to analyse instutions, power and ideology, we need to stop the slide into relativism which much discourse theory, and post-structuralism generally, encourages. We need some sense of the real to anchor our understanding of the dynamics of discourse. I turn to this question next.

Chapter 2

Realism, inside and outside texts

John Lister (*Socialist Outlook* No 14) says 'thoughts ... are material things ...'. They are not. Matter is that which exists independently of thoughts. There is no other definition. If thoughts are matter, how can matter exist independently of them? To say that thought is material is no better than saying matter is 'mental', and turns materialism into a nonsense. Both say 'matter and thoughts are the same stuff'. Cliff Slaughter, Leeds. PS I must correct Mike Pearse's letter on the WRP. The WRP's crisis of 1985 was not 'terminal'.

(Slaughter, 1989: 33)

Is discourse 'real', and is discourse analysis picking up 'real things'? How do discourses relate to the 'real world'? If we changed discourse, would that change the order of things? These questions frame and trip up critiques and defences of discourse-analytic research. There are old debates at work here, longstanding positions, in discourse, being rehearsed, and it is important to acknowledge the way two of the most important of these bear down on those of us who are trying to disentangle ourselves from the confused mess of traditional psychology and social science.

The first debate revolves around an ontological problem (to do with the nature of beings and things) with political consequences for how and where we direct our energies to understand and change the world. The two key opposing positions are materialism, in which everything that exists depends on matter, a real world, and idealism, in which ideas are independent and creative of the things we think are real. A materialist position entails a thorough scepticism about spiritual explanations of phenomena (archetypes, gaia, gods and so forth) and looks to an evolutionary account of the development of the material preconditions for language and thought. Interpretation here is only the prelude to a process of active engagement with real structures and attempts to change them. For a materialist, discourse must be related to the material world and discourse analysis must be connected in some way to other scientific modes of investigation. An idealist position, on the other hand, either leads to universalist accounts of the order of things, in which spiritual arrangements in hidden realms explain our experience, or to relativism, in which the power of thought to create things means that there is nothing more real than our different accounts, stories and theories. Instead of trying to change the world, the point is merely to reinterpret it. For an idealist, discourse is an independent and creative force, and science is just another discourse.

The second debate concerns an epistemological problem (to do with the nature and source of knowledge) with a more specific academic remit, but no less political consequences for how we defend a form of research which is able to, at least, empower those we study. The key opposing positions are brutally simplified here, but these are the ways ideas from the past weigh down like nightmares on the minds of those living in psychology now. On the one hand, behaviourism sustains the positivist science world-view and empiricist method in which only things that can be observed are worth studying (and anything that is worth studying can be measured). Language, discourse, in the crasser formulations of this view, is merely verbal behaviour. At the other side stands humanism, an umbrella term for the different alternative approaches which value varieties of experience and understanding (which are not reducible to correlations and statistical tests). It is within this alternative humanist strand that the turn to language during the crisis in social psychology has given birth to discourse analysis.

A problem is that these debates hook into one another. The positions seem to map onto each other. Competing materialist and idealist discourses here become tangled up with behaviourist and humanist discourses. This tangle has had the effect of pulling radicals in psychology in different surprising directions. There are two traps here. On the one hand, a first trap, there is a strong temptation for some to hold firm to a materialist view, to equate idealism with humanism, and to end up defending some version of traditional behaviourist psychology. While there are politically radical behaviourists, this route often leads to a sharp split between a critical position and a simple dehumanising academic or clinical psychological practice. On the other hand, a second trap some radicals are just as keen to adopt an anti-positivist stance, to equate behaviourism with materialism, and to end up being sucked into some version of idealism. Again, there are humanist action researchers into empowerment, but this route also all too often leads to passive, cynical and ultimately obstructive views of politics.

The mistaken idea that discourses create all we know and could know, all there is, falls into and fuels that second trap. It is not surprising that there is a 'worried about the real' discourse now which circulates among discourse analysts and their critics, and it is necessary to clear some way through two positions which are reproduced in speculations about the nature of the 'objects' that discourses contain: (i) one position is that things which become objects of discourse then exist only inside texts. To say this would be to adopt an extreme 'linguistic realist' argument, a current code phrase for relativism, here idealism; (ii) an alternative line, that things have no reality in discourse because things 'really' exist only outside texts, is pursued by extreme brute empiricists keen to reduce phenomena to observable behaviour. Neither of these positions is right.

It is clear that we need some way of talking about real things to ground discourse analysis, a materialist view sensitive to the powers of discourse which develops a critical realist position for psychology. In this chapter I will first of all briefly outline the bare bones of a realist position, and then, second, go on to relate this to ways of understanding the powers of discourse. In the third section I will turn to the ways in which a realist view of discourse could connect with conceptions of social structure and then, in the final section, address questions of change. First, then, realism.

REALISM

There are four features of the new realist position that has emerged in psychology in the last two decades (Manicas and Secord, 1983). These features effectively distil the realist philosophies of science elaborated by Harré (1970, 1986b) and then, in a critical realist fashion, by Bhaskar (1978, 1989).

The first point concerns ontology, the nature or, better, the natures of things. This point immediately addresses some of the concerns of humanists, for a realist view focuses on the manner in which things are complex composites of interacting structures. For example, a human being as a thing is a complex of biological structures, and this complex is able to move, speak, monitor movements and speech and also engage in a 'second-order' monitoring of the monitoring. The statement in the 'ethogenic' new-paradigm literature that we should 'for scientific purposes treat people as if they were human beings' (Harré and Secord, 1972: 84) flowed, in part, from a concern with the particular powers of second-order monitoring creatures. It is in the nature of a human being that it is reflexive, one of the powers with which it is endowed by virtue of its structure. The speech (and other communication) of a human being is structured into language(s) such that when groups or networks are formed an individual can move in and out of them, sharing all or part of the rules and tacit knowledge that hold them together. The study of a social world, then, cannot proceed by breaking it down into bits, into individuals. Explanations of the powers of these structures then need to address the way a complex works at a particular level. It is not possible to explain, or explain away, a pattern of behaviour by breaking it up into smaller bits. This is why people, by virtue of their nature, resist a reductionist account.

The second point is to do with epistemology, what we can know and how we know it. Scientific laws concern, and should concern, the causal properties of structures, and here it is necessary to make a distinction between, on the one hand, statistical probabilities which may merely pick up some connections or correlations, and, on the other hand, the way in which the powers of things are understood as possibilities or potentials. In this second sense, scientific laws are attempting to express patterns which occur and to picture the tendencies of things to act or react in particular ways. In some of the physical sciences it is possible to construct almost closed systems (test-tubes and suchlike) in which the tendencies of materials in different conditions can be studied, and the powers of those materials, their natures, described. Even in the physical sciences, however, factors such as gravity make a complete closed system impossible. It is necessary, then, to have theories about these operations under hypothetical conditions of complete closure. In the human sciences, closed systems exist only in the fantasies of hardened positivists. The theories we have about human nature can specify powers, but many of these powers can be exercised only by virtue of the engagement of a human being with others. Different, higher-level, rule-governed social worlds or communities are, in turn, not closed but open systems. All patterns of human interaction can only exist, as it were, in a state of uneven and combined development with those around them.

The third point revolves around questions of moral/political concern in knowledge, the way knowledge is structured. For a critical realist, the role of theory is crucial not only in the way it structures phenomena (and facilitates the identification and description of structures) but also in the apparatus of science. Knowledge, including scientific knowledge, is historically produced but aims to represent the world outside. There is a tension here. On the one hand, scientific knowledge employs rational criteria which have been developed in particular ways in particular cultures with varying views of rationality. On the other hand, there is an appeal to rationality because there is a world existing independent of experience. This means that scientific knowledge is at once historically bounded, provisional, and is also practical, true. This tension is not to be resolved (as if it were a problem), for it is actually one of the conditions for the production of knowledge. The empiricist fantasy of falsification as the simple knock-out criterion for saying which facts are incorrect tries to resolve that tension. For a realist, the way knowledge 'represents', works in the world can be both right as an overall research programme and wrong in specific details. There is no one-to-one relationship between a description and what it describes.

The fourth point concerns practice. The issue is to do with the connection between prediction and control on the one hand, and the relation between explanation and discipline on the other. The problem of creating closed systems is a largely technical one in the physical sciences, though one which gives rise to a lot of rhetoric about replicability (e.g., Potter and Mulkay, 1985). For the human sciences, the problem is both technical and deeply political. Because structures interact with those they are a part of, and with others, it is not possible to predict social behaviour at any level without controlling it. An abstract way of putting this point is to say that it is possible to make explanation and prediction symmetrical only under conditions of complete closure. A more concrete way of expressing it is to say that explanations of human behaviour can work only if there is the possibility of constructing closed systems in which there are no points of influence from without or resistance from within. Complex dehumanising social relationships are the prerequisite for controlled behaviour, and positivist psychology. The pity is that much positivist psychology does work, and this is, in part, because, once particular social arrangements are in place, they then operate as relatively enduring structures with their own knowable causal properties.

These four features of realism – the nature of things as complex structures, the use of theories about their tendencies under conditions of closure, the nature of rational knowledge as presupposing a world independent of experience, and the relationship between explanation and prediction – usefully provide a means for understanding the powers of discourse and the relationship between discourse and social structure, as I will go on to show.

POWERS OF DISCOURSE

Discourse (language organised into sets of texts) and discourses (systems of statements within and through those sets) have a power. To say this is not to attribute agency to a system, but simply to acknowledge constraining and productive forces. There are forces of institutional disadvantage and division, for example, which do not flow from individual intentions, and the phenomena of power and ideology need not be traced to conspiratorial machinations. To understand the powers and dynamics of discourse here we do not have to go outside the texts to hidden authors. In some cases (such as conspiracy theories) it would be dangerous to attempt to do so. It is necessary to focus on language as a structured system in its own right, and discourse analysis unravels the conceptual elisions and confusions by which language enjoys its power. It is implicit ideology critique. But there is also more than language, and discourse analysis needs to attend to the conditions which make the meanings of texts possible. It may be useful to conceive of things (in the broadest sense of the word) as being endowed with one of three possible 'object statuses', in one of three possible categories (but with many things appearing, in different forms, in more than one of the categories).

Ontological object status

There is, first of all, the realm in which things have ontological status. There are material conditions for the production of thought, and these include, though not in the way that reductionists would have it, the 'biological bases of behaviour', molecules, cells, neural networks, brains. When we are specifying such bases for thought we have to take care that the autonomy of this realm is not overrated. Thought, for example, is an attribute of beings embodied in, interacting with the world. This is why computer 'intelligence' cannot replicate the nature of thought (Dreyfus, 1967). Further, the nature of memory is largely a function of relationships, communities, and requires the material existence of many bodies structured into positions where habitual communication is possible (Middleton and Edwards, 1990). For a realist, such as Bhaskar (1989), such things belong to an 'intransitive' realm of physical structures endowed with particular powers. Much of the 'practical' sphere that Harré (1979) describes is made up of things which have ontological status.

The first realist point about the nature of things as complex structures is relevant here. A threefold problem arises in the way such things are understood by traditional psychology. Not only does brute empiricism: (i) try to reduce phenomena to a biological level as if it were the only material basis; and (ii) claim that things with ontological status can be directly known, unmediated by the structured relationships that a researcher is herself part of; but it also (iii) refuses to understand the particular natures of the objects it studies, treating, for example, groups as if they were people, people as if they were brains. It is not possible to describe or replicate precisely behaviours and responses, or to say, as some social psychologists have in critiques of discourse analysis, that it should 'demonstrate its superiority in dealing with the same phenomena and issues that concern social psychologists' (Abrams and Hogg, 1990: 219). We are not dealing with the 'same phenomena'.

Epistemological object status

There is no simple correspondence between things with ontological status and the things we have given meaning to, talk about, know about. Here, objects are on the edge of or have entered discourse, and things known are in a second sphere. These are things with epistemological object status. This does not mean that the things known, experienced through discourse, are not also endowed with ontological object status, but the point is that for a knowledge to exist, ontological object status is not enough. For a realist, it is not possible to obtain knowledge about things with only ontological status, those in the intransitive realm, without a pre-existing array of knowledge (and techniques) which lie in this second 'transitive' realm (Bhaskar, 1989).

The second two points of a realist view are relevant here. The point that it is necessary to use theories to picture the tendencies of things under hypothetical conditions of closure necessitates an historical account of the growth of knowledge. Here Kuhnian and Lakatosian descriptions (which are concerned with paradigm revolutions and research programmes) of assumptions which frame and drive the development of science give to the realist account a sensitivity to the social grounds of knowledge as material grounds. The point that systems of rational knowledge presuppose a world independent of experience draws attention to the need for (i) a form of relativism which respects the different and provisional culturally bounded explanations of the nature of things (and what things there are) which does not slide into (ii) the Nietszchean perspectivism of high post-structuralists for whom there are only ever competing stories. The first, (i) relativism, can also be grounded in the assumption that there is a real outside discourse which we are trying to understand (and in rules of discourse which value forms of argumentation, rhetorical debate about the real). The second, (ii) perspectivism, values only the struggle of different versions and forms of resistance in which appeals to rational criteria are seen as mere tactics to get one version into a dominant position (Descombes, 1980).

Moral/political status

Harré's (1979) 'expressive' order includes the knowledge we have of things, but I also want to mark out a third realm which is within the expressive order, within discourse, in which things have a moral/political status. Much talk about psychological phenomena is ideologically loaded such that objects such as 'intelligence', 'race', 'attitudes', etc., can be called into being, and thus given a 'reality'. In this third realm of things with a moral/political status, and it is a realm we cannot wish away (it is necessary to human society), we can always remind ourselves that such objects are being advanced for strategic reasons – we can treat them 'as if' they were there. Discourses and texts, having emerged from the third realm, now have epistemological status for some analysts, a status which is contested by others (e.g., Potter et al., 1990).

The fourth point made by realists, that concerning the relationship between explanation and prediction, is relevant here, for it is not possible to produce knowledge without being implicated in some way with political matters. The conditions of complete closure, for example, which guarantee a knowledge of human activity have been traced historically to the emergence of systems of control and surveillance. Foucault (1977), for example, describes the way that the regulation of prison populations, and then the population outside prisons, forged a link between prediction and control. Many of the phenomena observed by experimental psychologists are produced under conditions of enforced physical closure, in which the replication of those phenomena is necessarily predicated on the disempowerment of 'subjects' outside the laboratory.

There are two general related issues which arise from the notion that there is a third realm of objects with moral/political status. The first is that the (second) epistemological realm contains 'objects' of knowledge which are derived both from research into the ontological realm (with much of the translation in the modern world in this respect conducted by science) *and* from the objects produced in the moral/political sphere (with much of this translation process functioning as the production of fake intransitive material). The epistemological status of things, then, is often contested because such things pretend to represent the real (they derive from objects that really exist) when they actually merely represent items constructed in a political rhetoric (they derive typically from ideological pictures of the real). Take the notion of 'schizophrenia', for example, which has a status as an object of knowledge (epistemological), which is now supposed to rest in chromosome 5 (ontological) but which is actually distilled from debates in medical psychiatry (moral/political).

The second issue is that the moral/political realm reflects, and reproduces, dominant cultural forms of thought. Here it is not only that social arrangements become (relatively) enduring structures, but that we account for those structures and the causes of things in particular ways. In higher education and research, for example, there is a dynamic towards individual choice in which a range of forces (companies, local authorities, students, parents) are encouraged to determine what is taught (and researched) in the academic institutions. Deliberate policy decisions make places of education into self-governing corporate bodies, but the motivating forces for the transformation of academic issues into matters susceptible to a cost-benefit analysis seem to be the newly 'empowered' consumers. In a sense, this is true, but the nature (and 'powers') of individuals at any time flow not so much from their 'attitudes' or 'motivations' (which they then 'communicate' to others), but from the overall ideological context. We can tease apart that context through analysis of the discourses (of 'choice', 'individualism', 'efficiency') which set the ground rules for action. People 'make' discourse, but not in discursive conditions of their own choosing.

Relations between the three realms

There are three further points about the relationship between object status in the three realms. The ways in which things appear in material form, as knowledge, and as politically contested phenomena (and sometimes all at once) is the source of much confusion and ideological mystification.

A first point is to do with the way brute empiricism in traditional psychology seems to be comfortable only with either/or categories, and so treats the objects it conjures into existence as real in the way everything else is real. There is a continual appeal to the real, but it is a fantasised 'real' which owes a lot to individualism (with the 'individual' as an object brought into discourse as a moral/political object). It is *not* possible to discover meanings, for example, by going to the real 'source', for 'communication' is *not* the transfer of 'intentions' from one individual head to another (Easthope, 1990). To translate terms from discourse analysis into 'dependent variables' and suchlike would simply replace a focus on the organisation of language with the traditional attempts to define, predict and control 'behaviours', 'cognitions', etc. (things which are not really there).

The argument has been advanced that 'everyday human activities do not just *appear* vague and indefinite because we are still as yet ignorant of their true underlying nature, but that they are *really* vague' (Shotter, 1990a: 9). Reductionism appeals to the real, but its objects are called into being in the moral/political sphere, and are made to operate 'as if' they were true (as part of the apparatus of regulation which is the psy-complex). This is not to say that we do not need 'models of the person' compatible with a discourse approach (and I take up this question in Part III of this book), but discourse analysis is mainly concerned with the ways in which such 'objects' arose and the functions they serve in language and social relations.

Second, it should be clear that the (re)definition of a field of study by discourse analysis as consisting of 'texts' and 'discourses' should not necessarily lead to us, as experimental social psychologists have charged (Abrams and Hogg, 1990), being unable to believe that there is anything else outside language. This accusation also flows from the problem positivist psychologists have with a flexible, fuzzy sense of reality. When something can be interpreted (and so becomes a text) it does not dissolve and lose all other object status. When experimental social psychologists define their object of study, they want to see it in all places – claiming, for example, that 'social behaviour can occur everywhere, including a crowded subway' (Deaux and Wrightsman, 1984: 5). Even they need not wish away everything else as if it did not exist, though it does sometimes appear that they are tempted by this wish.

It is true that to talk of discourses as if they were things capable of intersecting, overlapping, positioning subjects can also lead to an abstraction and reification of theoretical constructs, constructs which are often politically loaded. The risk is worth taking, for it is crucial that we hold to some conception of the *difference* between discourses, and show how contests between different structures of meaning operate as part of the architecture of society. This happens as we move beyond 'common sense'. Just as there are different discourses, there are dominant and dominated cultures, different 'common senses'. To identify a discourse is to take a position, and the ability to step outside a discourse and to label it in a particular way is a function of both the accessing of dominant cultural meanings *and* the marginal (critical) position which the researcher takes (within or alongside another discourse or sub-culture or 'common sense').

There is a third point which concerns the importance of the setting for the operation of discourses: the way different settings give rise to different meanings, and the position of the researcher in the construction of those meanings (Sherrard, 1991). Here, it is important to note that for traditional psychologists to point to 'situational factors' as part of an attempt to devalue discourse research (e.g., Abrams and Hogg, 1990) is to repeat the mistaken assumption that the things a psychologist studies are discrete entities which interact with one another in, at least potentially, predictable ways. It would be possible to ask questions about differences in discourse in different circumstances, but such questions should be framed in terms of the conditions for the employment of different discourses and their intersection at different subject positions in institutions governed by relations of power and ideology.

It is in this context, of practice, that the issue of 'empowerment' could seriously be addressed, for it is only when the wider context is understood that one gets a sense of how particular discourses reproduce a dominant culture. Just as certain objects are called into being, given a moral/political status, then researched (given epistemological status) and treated as if they really are there (as if they had ontological status), so, as a critical response, certain objects can be studied as objects (solely, perhaps) of a discourse and thereby be deconstructed. Here, the researcher is caught up in moral/political choices concerning the reproduction and transformation of discourses. These choices also concern the reproduction and trans-formation of relationships with research participants (Bhavnani, 1990).

To move beyond traditional psychology, beyond an obsession with 'facts' about things as if they were all of the same kind, beyond an inability to believe that things could both be inside and outside texts and beyond a limited notion of situations as context for behaviour, is also to move into the realm of power and ideology. The relationships which frame discourse research are part of wider social structures, and our understanding of those structures is intimately linked with our understanding of change.

STRUCTURE

There are many notions of social structure. Four concepts of social structure have been usefully outlined recently (Porpora, 1989), and I will briefly mention some of the implications of each, spending a little longer on a realist account. These four concepts are hotly debated, as one would expect, in sociology, and they have direct relevance to a discourse-analytic psychology.

A first view is one that is most directly compatible with tacit theories of the social in orthodox psychology. Here, social structures are simply patterns of behaviour which are stable enough to be measured and predicted. There is no such thing as 'social class', 'culture' or the 'state'. There is no such thing as society. There are only individual men and women. Even the family is a collection of individuals behaving in predictable ways. In this account, and this is what most psychologists do as easily as breathing, we are invited to adopt a 'microviewpoint', look at 'microrepetition' of 'micro-behaviors' in 'micro-interaction' in 'microsituations', engage in 'microtranslation' (Collins, 1981). If we adopted this account, it would be virtually impossible to do discourse analysis, for discourses are structured sets of terms, tropes, metaphors, structures which are realised when they are used, but are more than 'micro-verbal-behaviour'. This account is so determinedly reductionist that it really has no account of social structure.

This view is mirrored in traditional sociology by a second account which treats structure as a system of regularities which have reality as 'social facts'. Because the regularities are there to be found inde-pendently of the conceptions of social structure used by individuals, they can be described in an objective (and quantifiable) way. This view, which flows from a Durkheimian tradition, does not have much to say about the activities of individuals, and deals with that issue by splitting 'science' into a type which studies social structure, sociology, and that which studies individual behaviour and minds, psychology (Parker, 1987a, 1989a). This account is positivist, and represents some of the worst 'anti-humanist' features of orthodox structuralism in which persons are simply ciphers of systems of meaning. Apart from devaluing the reflections, choices and struggles with the organisation of discourse that an individual does engage in, this notion of structure would have us believe that discourse 'analysis' would be only an objective matter, when it does also always require moral/political choices about terminology, positions and effects of identifying particular discourses.

One middle way through these first two accounts would be to adopt something akin to a third 'structurationist' position advanced by Giddens (1979). There are strong echoes of this position in the new social psychologies which look to some system of rules (of which no one individual is wholly cognisant) while respecting the accounts and agency of persons employing those rules as resources for acting out the dramas of social life (Harré, 1979). Social structure here is seen as the collective rules and resources which give a sense and pattern to action. This position is close, almost close enough, to the realist accounts I described earlier, for Giddens (1979), describing norms independent of individual choice, and Harré (1983), identifying primary structures of self and identity, are concerned with causal mechanisms. Discourse analysis linked to this tradition would be able to connect its description of a system of meanings with individual twists and transformations of those meanings by human agents.

However, the coercive reality of social structures, in this view, is not quite marked strongly enough. Giddens, for example, as Porpora (1989) points out, takes care to insist that social structures always rest on the tacit knowledge of individual participating agents. Such structures are culturally given, and have a power to frame what people may do, but they are not materially rooted in conditions of life, conditions which a person may never understand. In recent forays into discourse theory, Harré has adopted a similar cautious position: 'there are only actual conversations, past and present ... whatever concretely happened before, and ... human memories [of them] ... form both the personal and cultural resources for speakers to draw upon in constructing the present moment' (Davies and Harré, 1990: 44). The problem is that this 'immanentist' view would prevent an historical analysis of the development of discourses and the ways they meet to confirm or challenge structures of oppression outside memories of what concretely happened before.

The fourth position, that of critical realism (e.g., Bhaskar, 1989), is concerned to allow analysis to move beyond, outside, versions of intersubjective reality. The realist conception of social structure offers a version of materialism which takes account of different senses of reality, and of reality outside sense. Alongside the material basis for, potentials for, and constraints on action that are rooted in biology (Timpanaro, 1980), there are systems of relationships and positions which make certain actions and accounts possible, and some impossible. The category of ontological object status here includes the physical location of bodies in space. In a capitalist economy, for example, industrial workers are physically located for much of the time together with others, and certain types of collective action make sense. In patriarchal societies in the West, women are physically located in homes for much of the time and certain types of collective action do not make sense. In a world organised by structures of imperialism, victims outside and inside the industrial centres can only act, accept, or resist, in particular ways.

Bhaskar (1989) argues that if we are to call some set of beliefs 'ideological', then this must be because we are asserting that they are necessary in some way. We have to account for the reasons why such beliefs may be held. Ideological beliefs are not superficial or irrelevant; they are part of the very structures we want to understand.

When we want to understand the function of particular discourses, the way they position their subjects in relations of contempt and respect, of domination and subordination or of oppression and resistance, we pass quickly and ineluctably from conceptual critique to social critique. It is one of the peculiar characteristics of social science, as Bhaskar points out, that the explanation that we give of structures, insofar as they give rise to illusory beliefs, entails criticism and then the transformation instead of the reproduction of those structures:

> In the full development of the concept of ideology, theory fuses into practice, as facts about values, mediated by theories about facts, are transformed into values about facts. The rule of value-neutrality, the last shibboleth of the philosophy of social science, collapses, when we come to see that values themselves can be false.
>
> (Bhaskar, 1989: 87)

This model of social structure, then, is one in which people are unaware much of the time of the conditions in which they act. However, the realist view does not explain away the activities of individuals as active agents, dissolving them into sets of biologically based or conditioned behaviours or as subject positions in discourse. The ways in which the social world may be opaque to the most skilled and reflexive have been described as follows: 'activities may depend on or involve (a) unacknowledged conditions, (b) unintended consequences, (c) the exercise of tacit skills, and/or (d) unconscious motivation' (Bhaskar, 1989: 4). Whilst the images of individuality, responsibility and autonomy which post-structuralists describe as part of the disciplinary and confessional symbolic architecture of the dominant culture in the West do become bizarrely internalised and so self-fulfilling (Foucault, 1977, 1981), a realist view sees in those very capacities to reflect and remake the self the powers to change it. Because of the existence of society as something that stands always already there in relation to persons, it is not possible to say that we create society, rather we must either *reproduce* or *transform* it (Bhaskar, 1989).

CHANGE

As we confront the structures of the social, we have to reflect on why it might be that the use of alternative discourses does not lead automatically to alternative social forms. There are a number of reasons. I will discuss four and, in the process, trace some ways in which the real is mediated level upon level by discourses, and always by discourses which never fully escape the material conditions in which they are reproduced and transformed.

A first and important one is the role of direct physical coercion. One, sometimes neglected, aspect of the development of post-structuralism is the resurrection of Nietszchean ideas of struggle underlying and informing language. Foucault, for example, argues for a genealogy of relations of force in which the role of language is secondary to threatened or actual violent conflict: 'The history which bears and determines us has the form of a war rather than that of a language: relations of power, not relations of meaning' (1980: 114). Billig *et al.* (1988: 161) cite a later point in this passage (in a different translation) where Foucault refers to the 'violent, bloody and lethal' reality of conflict which is hidden by studies which focus on 'the calm Platonic form of language and dialogue' (Foucault, 1980: 115). It is necessary to have the physical possibility to develop new discourses. For many women, for example, the family is a site of physical coercion where it is simply not possible to speak. In Central America, for example, coercion is structured into the operation of dictatorships such that the personal is politicised, and so immediately becomes caught up in forms of war. The real always lies on the edge of discourse, making some moves in language games impossible.

A second block on the development of alternative forms lies in the material organisation of space, and the closing of spaces where certain forms of talk can be practised and elaborated. Ways of talking take hold when it makes sense, or when there are sub-communities which are organised such that alternative ideas make sense. It is necessary to have the space to develop new discourses. It is possible to develop new forms of therapeutic and political reflection, for example, in already constituted spaces such as religious buildings in Central America or Palestine (though the weight of clerical power and ideology also squeezes popular discourses here in progressive and reactionary directions). Another example is to be found in the way higher education institutions function as spaces for students away from the family for the exploration of alternative forms of sexuality. Texts are available (written, spoken), and there are discourses around which make sense in a way they could not 'at home'. There is a sense in which we should look for the meaning of a discourse only in its *use*, and certain discourses can be used only in certain places. The material organisation of space and the structure of institutions which hold and divide space, then, is a real force which frames discourse.

A third block lies in the habitual, physical orientation of the individual to discourse of different kinds, the problem of breaking from the past, either in the form of 'tacit skills', understood through ecological psychology perhaps (a line I pursue in Chapter 5) or in the struggle against 'unconscious motivation', defences such as resistance understood using psychoanalysis (an approach I discuss in Chapter 6). Either way, it is necessary to have the *break* to develop new discourses. Leaving aside the psychoanalytic model for the moment, one example would be the abrupt break from home and the immersion in student politics (politics in a wider sense than exposure to union hacks), and the sudden enforced assumption of new rules, new repertoires. Another example, on a slightly larger scale, is the break from the past that occurs with forms of revolution. If the critical realists are right, then such sudden breaks are necessary for the elaboration of new discourses, for such elaboration on the bones of an old social structure is impossible for the body politic to bear for long. Here, the notion of 'interpretative repertoire' does have an edge over the term 'discourse', for it can catch the way a speaking body is engaged in action as it follows the tracks of dominant representations of the world. The behavioural aspect to patterns of speech and the 'reading' of texts is ingrained habit. The real body, bent in a variety of postures of deferment and position in different discourses, is such that only a shock, a break can release the potential for the development of new repertoires.

The fourth block on change is that one which is focused on in studies of discourse which describe the positioning of selves, or the constitution of subjectivity in language (and here psychoanalytic accounts are often brought in to supplement a post-structuralist approach). The sense of the possibilities of change is relayed by discourses, for example, which position the 'subject' as being able to take on new roles. More to the point, the sense of exhaustion and despair in the face of direct threat or institutional sanctions is fed by discourses which relay the moral that things can never be changed and it is unrealistic to try. Both the hope and the hopelessness are reproduced and transformed in discourse as we engage, for example, in readings of other events in which change has happened. The Sandinistas seizing power also supported discourses in which oppressed subjects and those in solidarity read (and experienced) a narrative of change, liberation. Their defeat reproduced discourses in which the world would never change and individuals should content themselves with little narratives containing passive pliable subjects (in which they experienced themselves as those subjects). The meanings of representations of places outside the dominant culture of the West are informed, in this example, by an array of discourses which either excuse or condemn oppressive regimes, and the struggle for political solidarity has to include the elaboration of discourses of resistance. Here again, alternatives are premissed on a change in real conditions outside texts. The articulation of counter-discourses occurs in the *material* spaces (enclosed free areas, different relationships, the reading of new texts) which open in the gaps and contradictions in discourse and in the real.

The realist view of social structures is important not only for theoretical reasons, but also, and this is where the stance becomes 'critical realist', in the prospects for change that flow from it. Discourse analysis is implicit ideology critique, because the position of the researcher is reflexive. When there is attention to the dynamics of discourse linked to social structures this reflexivity can be grounded so issues of ideology and value become explicit. Different discourses carry with them different prescriptions for social relations, and those alternative discourses that both re-describe and provide a critical distance from language and power are also the basis for alternative social relations, alternative societal forms.

The notion that social structure is a precondition for discourse means that discourse analysis must draw on other theoretical and empirical work which uncovers the material basis of oppression (capitalism, colonialism, patriarchy). The mistaken idea that discourses are as real as anything, or everything, else is a crucial one to tackle, for versions of discourse theory are currently wreaking havoc within traditionally materialist political frameworks. The delusion that the world has arrived at the end of history and culture has settled into a postmodern condition has pulled not a few radicals away from any kind of ideology critique into varieties of 'post-Marxism' (Laclau and Mouffe, 1985). More worrying, perhaps, is that those fascinated by the power of discourse cut loose from any connection with a real outside texts are becoming the vehicles for the 'radical' expression of a purely pragmatic 'new realism' which has lost any desire to take underlying structures of oppression and resistance seriously. (To deny that thought is material, as in the mystifying quote at the beginning of this chapter, is no better.)

The downside of post-structuralism, one of the most rabid anti-realist approaches in the social sciences at present, is that it provokes an 'exhorbitation of language' at the expense of everything else, including politics (Anderson, 1983). There are equally serious political consequences which flow from analyses which proclaim the end of modernity and the dawn of a 'postmodern' age in which all the worst aspects of post-structuralism seem to have come 'true', written out over the whole of culture. These supposed cultural transform-ations are connected with economic and structural changes in the West, but the systems of reflection, despair and celebration over the changes are rooted in discourse. This means that if discourse analysis is to play a helpful part in cultural analysis it must attend to the formation of modernity and the current threats to the modern project of individual, social and political enlightenment. I turn to these matters in Part II.

Part II
Cultures

The analysis of texts has to be placed in cultural context, and an understanding of discourse dynamics developed in an account of tensions and transformations in culture. The two chapters which make up this second part of the book draw upon the realist argument outlined in the previous chapter. The 'metanarratives', or dominant discourses, of modernity which are traced in Chapter 3 both permit, and close off, explanations of society and individual experience. These discourses can be connected with material changes in the organisation of space and bodies, and political responses to those changes.

The metanarratives of modernity are discourses which describe (and prescribe) 'truths' about individuals and social behaviour. I take one text in Chapter 3, a novel written at the beginning of the nineteenth century, and show how the discourses of science, progress and personal meaning are used. I show how the 'dilemmas' which these discourses set up are contested and resolved. As well as offering an example of a discourse analysis of literature, this exercise provides an opportunity for exploring the ways in which power and ideology are produced, maintained and challenged at a discursive level.

Our understanding of these changes is contrasted, in Chapter 4, with the turn to 'little stories' that current preoccupations with postmodernity encourage. It is possible here also to sketch the contours of the cultural context in which psychological research comes to focus on 'discourse'. Descriptions of postmodern culture have drawn attention to the decline of the wide-ranging discourses about individuals and society which arose at the beginning of the nineteenth century. Whilst I explain why the term 'postmodernity' is mistaken, I show how the postmodernism found in many social sciences has a reality, and has mixed effects on research. The discourse about discourse which discourse research reproduces, the thorough-going scepticism which it provokes and the reflexivity it advocates are manifestations of postmodernism. The chapter concludes by examining the ways in which reflexivity ostensibly bridges, and the way it actually intensifies, the *modern* gulf between the social and the individual.

Chapter 3

Novel narratives of modern times

Music, art and science. Now all of these things are essentially European.

(Margaret Thatcher, 1989)

There is an intimate and intriguing relationship between psychology and literature, for both disciplines provide pictures of action and experience and both claim to represent the truths of mental life. In different ways, reality claims are made by these scientific and artistic wings of Western culture, but attempts to make connections between the two have been made difficult by the stubbornly held assumptions of practitioners on the two sides: 'the causal, individualistic model of influence underlying traditional social psychology and the "truth and insight" model of writing which underlies traditional literary criticism' (Potter *et al.*, 1984: 51). However, it is possible to deconstruct the difference between psychology and literature once we move away from the obsessions with truth that govern the two areas. This process can also help us understand the dynamics of culture, tensions reproduced and transformed in discourse.

In literature, the development of post-structuralist theory has provided a powerful challenge to traditional views of writing. The literary text, or any text for that matter, was no longer seen as the product of creative genius (Eagleton, 1983). Barthes argued that 'The text is a tissue of quotations drawn from the innumerable centres of culture' (1977: 146). This opened the way for a treatment of even the most precious poetic expressions of the human spirit as discourse (Easthope, 1983). Post-structuralism has taken fast in a variety of academic disciplines ranging from English literature to psychology; with this theoretical approach it was possible to collapse art into popular culture, philosophy into literature and science into discourse. Any type of writing could be studied as a 'literary' form (Easthope, 1988).

In psychology, the turn to language through the new-paradigm challenge to laboratory-experimentation (Harré and Secord, 1972) has often involved a discussion of literary texts. Unlike the traditional psychologies which looked to literature as a repository of examples or confirmations of the truths discovered through proper empirical research (e.g., Ridgway and Benjamin, 1987), the approaches coming in the wake of, *and* templates for, the crisis in social psychology have looked to texts as exemplars of experience (e.g., Harré, 1983). The turn to discourse has further drawn attention to the constructive nature of literary language: 'Texts cannot be taken as straightforward descriptions of events, and events cannot be detached and analysed separately from the text' (Wetherell *et al.*, 1983: 377).

The relationship between literature and psychology has been articulated in readings of literary texts and psychological accounts in a way which challenges the notion that studies within the two disciplines have to be seen as mutually exclusive categories of work. There have been discussions, for example, of the relationship in such a way as: to give a description of the way gender is constructed as a category of experience within linguistic repertoires (Wetherell, 1986); to show how the self is displayed in the thriller genre (Back, 1989); and to illustrate the positioning of adult and child readers in relation to the discourse of radical fairy tales (Davies and Harré, 1990).

Deconstruction, part of the methodological armoury of post-structuralism, has also been used to treat social psychology as consisting of a series of detective, autobiographical and science fiction narratives (Squire, 1990a). It may be true that 'writing is the destruction of every voice, of every point of origin' (Barthes, 1977: 142). If so, psychology's attempt to locate problems inside individuals' heads is deeply problematic. This is not to say that the interrelationship between avant garde literary theory and psychology has been without problems (Parker, 1989a), but the connection has opened up fruitful contradictions within the different areas.

There are two other points around which these ideas are expressed and which direct our attention to a crucial connection between literature and psychology. The first is to be found in contemporary philosophy, in the influential argument that instead of believing that our accounts, including scientific accounts, are 'mirrors of nature', we should understand all knowledge as discursive, provisional, relative (Rorty, 1980). The second arises in cultural studies, in the argument that there is no such thing as society, there are only little stories told about it (Lyotard, 1984). These assertions, that we should now abandon the fetish for truth and recognise the essentially fictional nature of human existence, have implications for how we view the past and present. I will be dealing in this chapter with the development of *modern* notions of truth and their expression in literature. I take up the turn to little stories in postmodern visions of the social in the following chapter.

There may be no mirrors of nature in philosophy, science, psychology or literature, but there is a crucial sense in which the pictures in the texts which comprise these disciplines reflect one another within the dominant culture. The argument has been well made that '[t]he picture we gain from a text is not determined so much by some underlying experience of the author but by the arrangement and structure of the words in the text and their place in general cultural systems of meaning' (Potter *et al.*, 1984: 23). We move, with this argument, from a referential model (which always presumes some corresponding object outside the text in a one-to-one way) to a relational one (which looks at the way new meanings and 'objects' are formed in the text). As well as being relational, modern cultural systems of meaning can be understood as overarching knowledge structures meshed through with power (Parker, 1989b). Because these pictures and forms of knowledge are part of the symbolic architecture of the West, it is also useful to trace the way different 'ideas' have developed in particular texts in order to understand contemporary links between discourse and power.

In this chapter I will trace accounts of key psychological *phenomena* circulated in the discourses and texts of culture, and my references will be to some patches of literature, cultural analysis and political writing which inhabit Western culture. I aim to show that modern conceptions of the world have a history, that the discourses that relay those conceptions are contradictory, and that the dynamics which power and transform the contradictions are a necessary and progressive part of the modern enlightenment project. In the first section I will explore some of the pictures of this modern age. Then, in the second section, I will describe the discourses in one novel produced early on in this historical period. As well being a site for the operation of discourse, the novel is a site of critique, and in the third section of the chapter I will briefly draw attention to the ways in which modern discourses have developed and transformed themselves, the sense in which they are dynamic and contradictory. I will conclude with a description of the way connections between literature and psychology are being made in practice with processes of cultural and personal transformation.

MODERNITY

The historical period which frames the experience of the West now is that of modernity, sometimes termed 'the enlightenment' (e.g., Billig *et al.*, 1988). I shall use the terms 'modernity' and 'enlightenment' interchangeably here. According to Foucault (1970) the birth of modernity had involved a conceptual inversion of classical thought in three fields: in overall views of the world (philosophy); in theories about the source of knowledge (epistemology); and in notions of the self (ontology). The conceptual machinery of universal truth, science, and an emphasis on the immutable structure of the natural world as the source of self-understanding were displaced from centre stage. These dominant discourses belonged, it is said, to the previous 'classical age' (Foucault, 1970). As a consequence, the new modern ideas of 'relativism', 'common sense' and 'personal knowledge' appeared. These ideas percolated into academic disciplines at different rates, finding their way late into new-paradigm psychology at the beginning of the 1970s (Parker, 1989a). But, both literature and psychology as disciplines, as well as the common sense outside that informs them, carry with them the effects of the old as well as new ages: the new open liberal humanist ideas which make modernity so attractive contain within them reminders of the old classical world-views.

When we attempt to highlight the key features of the culture of modernity, the representations of the world and ourselves as organised through discourses of humanised science, progress and individual meaning, we find traces of past periods woven into them. It is here that 'tradition' is located. In the case of 'royalty', for example, as representation of all that is right about tradition, family and property, a sense of continuity is maintained by discourses around cultural icons, and they inform what we call 'attitudes' mistakenly located in individual heads (Billig, 1988a). It is those discourses that make *collective* memory and ideology possible (Billig,

1990b). Little surprise, perhaps, that the largest fascist group in Russia now is called 'Memory' (*Pamyat*). There is, incidentally, a semi-fascist fundamentalist Christian group in Latin America called 'Tradition, Family and Property' (Löwy, 1988). The dynamics of collective thought contain tensions in which we continually risk a regression of history as well as paths to progress. There is, as psycho-analytically informed cultural analysts of fascism in the Frankfurt School tradition said, a dialectic to the enlightenment (Adorno and Horkheimer, 1972).

It would be possible to develop Foucault's (1977, 1981) later accounts of modern networks of power, discipline and confession so that all discourse emerging in modernity appeared to be oppressive (e.g., Parker, 1989b). We should, however, be cautious here. Berman has argued that 'there is no freedom in Foucault's world, because his language forms a seamless web, a cage far more airtight than anything Weber ever dreamed of, into which no life can break. The mystery is why so many of today's intellectuals seem to want to choke in there with him' (1983: 35). Foucault is caricatured here, but the point is a good one, for many Foucauldians have come to the mistaken conclusion that there is no room any more, nor was there ever, for liberation. Berman's argument is part of a wider-ranging alternative discussion of modern culture, to which I will return below.

Culture is contradictory. We are often forced to acknowledge the presence of conflicting discourses in its texts, and it is this presence of contradiction which allows room for resistance, the refusal to respond within dominant meanings. We can see this contra-diction in the texts which appeared in the English language at the turn of the eighteenth century, at the beginning of modernity. Within discourse analysis, the collection of studies in *Ideological Dilemmas* has been useful in tackling this question head-on. First of all, the authors have focused on the 'historical dimension' of their topics, such as gender, health and prejudice, and 'sought to draw attention to the continuing ideological history of liberalism, and of the Enlightenment' (Billig *et al.*, 1988: 145). They provide a general characterisation of Western enlightenment thought as revolving round liberal individualism.

Second, they have insisted that 'ideology does not imprint single images but produces dilemmatic quandaries' (Billig *et al.*, 1988: 146). These quandaries contain possibilities for resistance, as well as the very conditions for 'thought', here seen as a social, argumentative process (Billig, 1987). While collective memory is the source of reactionary ideologies, it is also the accumulation of experience of progressive ideas (Middleton and Edwards, 1990). In the case of prejudice, for example, Billig *et al.* point out that it 'is to be dispelled when the underlying conditions, on which prejudice depends, are changed and the terms of present discussion are altered' (1988: 148). However, this does not mean the obliteration of the contested nature of conversation, of discourse. It is necessary, according to them, to provoke and support contradiction as an *end* as well as means, as an *enlightened* enlightenment.

MODERN NARRATIVES

The novel form represents one attempt, springing to life at the beginning of modernity, to enlighten a readership through processes of reflective narrative. Within that form, the conflicting discourses vying for supremacy in the new culture are well represented in *satire*. Modern satire stretches out versions of the social order, caricatures for moral effect, and represents a 'real' nature that is purported to lie within its victims. It presupposes a 'real' against which the reader might understand the images in the text. It represents positions in discourse in such a way that dilemmas, quandaries must be struggled with. Satirical representations are, for this reason, a crucial part of the literary and popular armoury of the modern age. Early examples of this genre are found in novels appearing at the beginning of the nineteenth century. One such satirical novel is Thomas Love Peacock's (1818) *Melincourt*. Within each of the categories of philosophy, epistemology and ontology, we witness modern discourses taking shape in the text.

Peacock, a close friend of the poet Shelley, wrote a number of novels in the early nineteenth century in which characters representing caricatured popular intellectual positions gathered at a country house and argued their positions while engaging in a series of adventures together. *Melincourt* is not untypical of his work, and Peacock sets the novel at Melincourt Castle, home of Anthelia Melincourt, a mysterious beautiful young woman. Among the characters converging on the castle are the rationalist Mr Fax, the humanist Sylvan Forester and his protégé Sir Oran Haut-ton. At one point in the story they make an expedition to visit a Mr Mystic, but this is but one *divertissement* in a romance which will end in marriage between Sylvan and Anthelia. I will trace through the three main discourses under the headings of philosophy, epistemology and ontology.

Philosophy

Views of the world, philosophies, are to be found in Peacock's novel clustered around preoccupations with science and nature. Mr Fax speaks for the scientific method as the route to true knowledge of the natural world and as the root of a solution to the problems of human society. It is no accident that he expresses an interest in both of these issues. With regard to the first, his claim that 'science is both morally and politically neutral' (717) gives an optimistic evolutionary sense to his belief 'in the progress of science and the rapid diffusion of intellectual light' (692). This itself demands the subordination of lower mental faculties and lower classes to 'the intellectual, which is the better part of human nature ... in a progress of rapid improvement, continually enlarging its views and multiplying its acquisitions' (693). Mr Fax, then, is the humean being who explains Mr Forester's vision of Anthelia Melincourt, for example, by way of the 'single mental principle' of 'the association of ideas' (679).

Apart from leading us to true knowledge, the other proclaimed benefit of scientific knowledge is its promise to provide the basis for the rational reorganisation of human society. Here Mr Fax is able to counter Mr Forester's vision of the original ideal healthy human being who coexists with nature, for which the 'rapid and sudden mutations of fortune are the inexhaustible theme of history, poetry and romance' (527). Mr Fax adapts his mathematics to Malthusian designs on 'the tendency of the population to increase beyond the means of subsistence' (527), and arrives at a solution: 'The remedy is an universal social compact, binding both sexes to equally rigid celibacy, till the prospect of maintaining the average number of six children be as clear as the arithmetic of futurity can make it' (527).

Together, then, Mr Fax and Mr Forester appeal to a natural progression. Whether 'feelings and poetical images are ... out of place in a calm philosophical view of human society' (526) as Mr Fax contends, or whether 'the qualities of the heart and of the mind are alone out of the power of accident' (551) as Mr Forester argues, is of secondary importance. Mr Forester speaks for the anthropomorphic spirit of modernity, though he does see the rise of industry as an evil:

'The mortality of a manufacturing town, compared with that of a mountain village, is more than three to one' (692). His dialogues with Mr Fax are intended to humanise the mechanisms of classical science Mr Fax supports. However, in some respects he still sees nature as calling for modern help, and the 'evil effects of the natural life' (692) include 'the coacervation of multitudes within the narrow precincts of cities, where the breath of so many animals, and the exhalations from the dead, the dying, and corrupted things of all kinds, make the air little better than a slow poison' (692). The new humanism Mr Forester hopes for, then, is easily drawn out and applied as but a gloss on Mr Fax's positivist position. Discourses of rational truth coexist with humanist relativist discourse.

Epistemology

Theories about the source of knowledge, epistemology, arise in the text in debates over what it is possible to know and how we can get to know it. When we turn to speculations as to the basis of knowledge, and the meanings of representation in human experience, we find Mr Forester's romanticism conflicting with the introspections of Mr Mystic. When both Mr Forester and Mr Fax are unable to see the grounds surrounding Mr Mystic's lodge because of the fog, they are angrily accused by him of being *'empirical psychologists*, and *slaves of definition, induction, and analysis*, which he intended for terms of abuse, but which were not taken for such by the persons to whom he addressed them' (668–9). For all three, of course, there is a potentially correct view of the world, and a true knowledge is possible and desirable. On certain crucial matters, however, Mr Mystic differs from his two friends for he differentiates, in keeping with the spirit of the new age, between *'objective* and *subjective reality*: and this point of view is *transcendentalism*' (669). The human being thus emerges as the locus of truth and creator of representations of the world and of the self.

Mr Mystic invites Mr Fax and Mr Forester to take a boat across a lake called the *'Ocean of Deceitful Form'* to the *'Island of Pure Intelligence'* where he lives (665). The fog which pervades the grounds of the lodge on the island, 'which he had laid out according to the *topography of the human mind*' (665), is only dispelled (and only dispelled for Mr Mystic) by the use of a *'synthetical torch*, which, according to Mr Mystic, *shed around it the rays of transcendental illumination*' (668). Against the positivism of Mr Fax, and the extension of his method into a vision of an organicist society governed by natural laws, to be described by 'the arithmetic of futurity' (527), Mr Mystic turns into the mind as the mirror of nature in which scientific knowledge is to be found reflected as personal truth. Against optimistic appeals to natural common sense and common human cause made by Mr Forester, Mr Mystic's vision is deliberately individualistic: 'The materials of political gloom will build the steadfast frame of hope' (670).

Mr Forester does hope to turn reason to the service of nature because he believes that original reason arises there, and so he contends that Mr Mystic is guilty of 'condensing in the human mind the vapours of ignorance and delusion' (672). Mr Mystic unwittingly recirculates the romantic writings of Coleridge. (Direct quotes from the poet are placed in Mr Mystic's mouth by Peacock and footnoted under the text.) He twists them around, and is able to make them mean what he likes. In this case they are used to resist all attempts at order, even ordered reform: 'Science classifies flowers. Can it make them bloom where it has placed them in its classification?' (671) Mr Mystic is, then, in employing this line of argument, acting as a herald of modernity (which he also reveals, in his reinterpretation of Mr Forester's romantic reforms, to be the age of kant). Scientific discourse exists here in tension with a discourse of common sense.

Ontology

Notions of the self, ontology, are marked out by the characters particularly carefully in discussions of possible distinctions between human and animal life. The alternative title of *Melincourt* is *Sir Oran Haut-ton*, and the sub-text of the novel concerns Mr Forester's attempt to get his friend, who is an oran outang, recognised as a human being. Sir Oran Haut-ton's 'prodigious physical strength, his uninterrupted health, and his amiable simplicity of manners demonstrate' (513), for Mr Forester, that his friend is 'a specimen of the natural and original man – a genuine facsimile of the philosophical Adam' (513). He has already made him a Baronet, and the next step is to have him elected to Parliament for a rotten borough. What is at stake here is a process of demarcation, in which the category of 'human being' is being redefined. While the old order had emphasised natural, and often supernatural, causes and models as the basis of human experience, the new age saw the phenomenon of the individual self emerge as the source of meaning and enlightenment. Political agency here is closely tied to criteria for distinguishing humanity from 'lower' animals. The problem that becomes intensified, as a necessary by-product, is how to decide what responsibilities, and rights to make meaning, should be attributed to human beings *alone*.

The attribution of causes, as a process embodied in a system of social rules embedded in discourse, changed rapidly in the course of a few centuries. Before the onset of the classical age (organised around the conceptual machinery of truth, natural science and an emphasis on external structures as the source of self-experience), the attribution of responsibility for criminal offences, for example, as codified in legal judgment, was regularly made to animals as well as to human beings. A lay court in France in 1386 tried and sentenced to death a sow which had killed a baby. It was dressed in breeches and jacket and then hung. In 1397 two herds of pigs were condemned to death. Three of the pigs had mauled a child, and their colleagues were tried as accomplices for squealing enthusiastically (though they were released at appeal). In this period a variety of animals were given elaborate trials with prosecution and defence witnesses. One of the most famous of defence counsels gained his legal reputation for securing the acquittal of a ferret on a technicality (Evans, 1906).

Mr Forester's attempt to admit Sir Oran Haut-ton to the realms of humankind is of a piece with his attempts to relieve human suffering and to accord human 'rights' to all. Hence the organisation of the 'anti-saccharine fête' to prevent the 'politically abominable' use of sugar as a commodity derived from slavery (646). The championing of the oran outang, then, was an issue not so much to do with who should not be excluded, but with how those who were to be *included* within the sphere of humanity as sovereign individuals should be attributed political rights and moral faculties. While Mr Forester failed in redrawing the boundaries between the animal and human spheres, he succeeded in reinforcing the conception of the self, as original and foundational, which provides an essential phenomenological support for the structures of modern culture.

Other languages of modernity

There are, of course, many more discourses threading their way through *Melincourt*. Anthelia Melincourt breaks from traditional gender roles in her striving for human sense, tolerance and meaning (her 'twin soul' is Mr Forester), but it is her abduction, her *absence*, which is the narrative pretext for the other assorted male characters to pursue their debates. There is a tension between a liberal and a reactionary ideology in the text, which is covertly resolved in favour of the latter when Anthelia and Mr Forester marry. Familial discourse gives a particular sense, and institutional form, to the nature of the harmonious relationship between a gentle man and, it turns out, a more than gentle (thoroughly feminine) woman.

A similar contradiction attends the public political activities of Mr Forester. While his saccharine boycott is part of a politically progressive liberal position, the context, the onset of imperialism, in which the oran outang came to be transported from the forests of Angola and studied as a form of African is necessarily left in silence. Colonialism is the precondition for this text to work, but it is only later on that a colonialist discourse becomes developed and contested as such. There are suppressed discourses which surface to the realms of political debate as modernity develops politically and allows the formation of explicit and recognised spaces of resistance to its oppressive forms. *Melincourt* carries then and now, but in different ways for different audiences, as much sexism and racism as many a modernist text.

A debate which the novel alludes to, and which is picked up again a century and a half later at what sometimes appears to be the end of modernity (where we are now, dear reader), concerns the nature of language and speech. A problem for Mr Forester is that Sir Oran Haut-ton cannot speak. He accounts for this lack by arguing that 'speech is a highly artificial faculty. Civilised man is a highly artificial animal' (521). Alongside this line of defence is the assertion that 'in the nation of the Orans ... drawing, as a means of communicating ideas, may be in no contemptible state of forwardness' (569). We are led to believe that underneath speech there is the more original substrate of 'communication'. This is not *only* caricature on Peacock's part, for Mr Forester's defence of the oran outang and his theories of language, speech and communication are copiously footnoted with references to contemporary early nineteenth-century debates as to the nature of the oran outang and the meaning of the animal's failure to speak.

'Speech' in Western discourse is conventionally accorded a privilege over 'writing' because it lies closer to thought, a privilege discussed in post-structuralist writing by Derrida (1983). However, there are different ways of unravelling, of deconstructing, of understanding the relationship between the pairs of that opposition. In Peacock's *Melincourt* at the birth of modernity there is an attempt to guarantee the humanity of a non-speaking being by attributing to him an ability to communicate which is more basic than speech. All communication can be resolved, according to Mr Forester's defence, into the level of *drawing*. So, Sir Oran Haut-ton's lively interaction with a tourist who is sketching is explained as being a natural response to the power of *representation*: 'his delight was excited by seeing the vast scene before him transferred so accurately into so small a compass, and growing, as it were, into a distinct identity under the hand of the artist' (570). As the discourse dynamics of modernity gathered pace, the relationship between language and experience was tangled further with the development of psychoanalysis, and now psychotherapy generally, as a 'talking cure'. The revival of psycho-analytic ideas in recent years would indicate that enlightenment may have changed rather than have simply run its course.

It is worth noting, in contrast, the more pessimistic post-Foucauldian forecasts. In this vision, now, at the supposed end of modernity, deconstructions carried out within the post-structuralist tradition are concerned with resolving the distinction in the other direction. Speech is dissolved into language, into the 'difference' of texts and discourses. This enterprise is just one 'expression' of the popularisation of the power of language that celebrants of 'post'-modernity promulgate (Lyotard, 1984), an issue I will address in the next chapter.

However, it is important first to locate the development of tensions within the discourses of modernity from its birth, for the existence of contemporary contradictory ideas and fashions can otherwise be inflated far beyond their historical significance. Although times change, we have to be clear in what ways they break from the past and in what ways they *continue* the dynamic of traditional discourses.

CHANGING NARRATIVES

The novel *Melincourt* reproduces the grand narratives of modernity, but we need to situate the development of those narratives. They are not static discourses overarching and informing *all* the things that can be said in Western culture. The very possibility of satire and of contradiction in Peacock's work indicates, as Billig *et al.* (1988) argue, that quandaries and dilemmas are an integral part of enlightened modern thought. In so far as the dominant discourses do inform the many ways in which we speak, they are fragmented, uncertain, contested. There is a dynamic at work in the way the narratives, as part of one optimistic movement, arose early in the modern condition, and the way they have splintered into a range of competing, more pessimistic world-views. Here I want to pursue this argument and temper an analysis of modern discourses informed by a Foucauldian framework with the descriptions offered by Berman in the book *All That Is Solid Melts Into Air* (1982).

Berman, sketches the development of a first phase of modernity, from the start of the sixteenth century to the end of the eighteenth, in which modern ideas were starting to gain a hold. It should be remembered that the very notion of the 'modern' was *developed*, not given, within the English language: 'Its earliest English senses were nearer our *contemporary*, in the sense of something existing now. . . . A conventional contrast between *ancient* and *modern* was established in the Renaissance. . . . *Modern* in this comparative and historical sense was common from lC16 [late sixteenth century]' (Williams, 1976: 174). For Berman, the second phase is powered by the cultural shocks of the French Revolution, and it is in this context that Peacock's narrative takes shape. Not only is history moving forward, but it requires a rational, scientific world-view to bring about an equal community in which each person realises their own capacities. Social (political) improvement is closely tied to individual (moral) improvement. Berman's 'third phase', the twentieth century, sees the spread of modernisation. Modernity is exported in technically sophisticated forms of colonialism, and, with the necessary links between 'enlightenment' and oppression, economic discipline and cultural resistance, modern ideas become fragmented and contradictory, for some to an unbearable degree.

This sense of fragmentation is now the cultural backdrop for the rise of a discourse analysis research programme which celebrates variability while trying to find meaning in the incompatible ways of talking which invade every text. The bits, structures of sense which we call 'discourses' or 'interpretative repertoires', are located by Berman (1982) in his evocation of the experience of modernity. The dynamic of the past, grand narratives of science, progress and individual enlightenment, impels us to make sense of a culture in which those ideas no longer seem to work. Modern built environments, for example, which promise to cut across cultural difference and unite all humanity give rise to an internally contradictory shared experience: 'it is a paradoxical unity, a unity of disunity: it pours us all into a maelstrom of perpetual disintegration and renewal, of struggle and contradiction, of ambiguity and anguish' (Berman, 1982: 15).

There is a passage from the *Communist Manifesto*, written in the midst of modern mid-nineteenth-century European political struggle, in 1848, which inspires the title of Berman's (1982) account, which explains that modern experience is rooted in the continual revolutions in production and innovations in marketing that are necessary for the bourgeoisie to exist:

> [U]ninterrupted disturbance of all social conditions, everlasting uncertainty and agitation. . . . All fixed, fast-frozen relations, with their train of ancient and venerable prejudices and opinions, are swept away, all new-formed ones become antiquated before they can ossify. All that is solid melts into air, all that is holy is profaned, and man [*sic*] is at last compelled to face with sober senses his real conditions of life and his relations with his kind.
>
> (Marx and Engels, 1965: 36–7)

In this account, cultural matters are rooted firmly in economic changes, changes which need to be explored using Marxism as a research programme within a realist framework (Bhaskar, 1989). Other accounts of the tensions within the modern age, which deliberately evoke the symbolic dynamics of culture and the coexistence of discourses from the past with those of the present, are to be found in writings on fascism. Fascism, as the ever-present underside of the dialectic of enlightenment, lies hidden within the discourses that comprise the processes of collective remembering (Middleton and Edwards, 1990). This, also a Marxist account, written in the 1930s, has relevance today:

> Today, not only in peasant homes but also in city skyscrapers, there lives alongside of the twentieth century the tenth or the thirteenth. A hundred million people use electricity and still believe in the magic power of signs and exorcisms. The Pope of Rome broadcasts over the radio about the miraculous transformation of water into wine. Movie stars go to the mediums. Aviators who pilot miraculous mechanisms created by man's [*sic*]

genius wear amulets on their sweaters. . . . Everything that should have been eliminated from the national organism in the form of cultural excrement in the course of the normal development of society has now come gushing out from the throat. . . . The programme of . . . illusions is . . . torn away from reality, and dissolved in ritualistic acts. . . . If the road to hell is paved with good intentions, then the avenues of the Third Reich are paved with symbols.

(Trotsky, 1933: 413–14)

There is a sense of menace highlighted here, lying within and underneath modern discourses, which is never brought to the surface in Peacock's writings. It is, perhaps, in more contemporary writers such as Pinter that this menace is expressed as an integral part of the text (Ashton, 1990). The historical descriptions given by Berman, Marx and Engels and by Trotsky, for example, are not informed by discourse analysis, and we can make sense of what they have to say without it. There are occasions when discourse analysis is not necessary or useful in helping us understand or evaluate texts (Burman, in press b).

The grand narratives of modernity explode at times of acute economic and political crisis, but the menace evoked in times of relative calm is just as telling. There are then occasions when we can draw on the understanding of culture that such writings about times of crisis provide to identify discourses in more innocent texts. Billig et al.'s (1988) argument that we need to attend to implicit meanings in discourse, and that this attention needs to be informed by historical, cultural and political scholarship, is particularly cogent here (Billig, 1988c). Take the following piece of text, for example, in the light of the previous one, and consider what it could mean.

There is a tiny church. Eight centuries of England lie buried around it. It allows a glimpse of an England that has not changed. Of course now there are roads, cars, planes, television. But there is, too, an England as she was: changeless in our fast-changing world.

(Michael Heseltine, 1990)

It is not necessarily on the grounds of authorial responsibility, the grounds traditionally ploughed by psychology and literary theory, that we should worry about such a quote. The images flow from the discourses which inhabit it, and from their contradictory modern dynamics.

DISCURSIVE CHANGES AND TEXTUAL PRACTICES

The changes in culture from the beginning of the nineteenth century
to the close of the twentieth have expressed and produced a
multitude of contradictory currents of thought. The form of language
itself as discourse is being interrogated and reworked at an increasing
pace, and not only in academic life. While the nature of the literary
canon and psychological theory has been undergoing a process of
upheaval, a correlative reflexive turn to language has been occurring
in the 'real' world. Two examples of this are the challenging of
conventional interpretations of literary texts and the use of
re-interpretation in therapeutic narratives.

The first example, the work of a small regional theatre group in
England, concerns the deliberate uses made of literature as *text* and
is just one expression of the reflexive study of post-colonial discourse
by some of its subjects. In *The Government Inspector Ala Afsur* by
Tara Arts Group (1989), Gogol's classic text is reworked as a piece of
theatre which challenges and re-presents received interpretations for
an audience in 'post-colonial Britain'. All quotes in this section are
from the programme leaflet which presents a reflexive commentary
on the performance. The reader of the play is also confronted, as
reader of the accompanying gloss on the play, with accounts of the
meanings which are being circulated and contested in Gogol's text.

The original play concerns the visit of a Moscow bureaucrat to a
remote provincial town where, through mistaken identity devices, the
attempts of the local officials and townspeople to impress and
manipulate the inspector highlight phenomena of oppression,
collaboration, corruption and resistance. The text has travelled to
India where it was translated many times into different Indian
languages and performed as a satirical display of colonial relationships between imperialism and the Third World. It returns to Britain,
performed in this production by first- and second-generation Asian
performers, having accumulated layers of conventions, 'each
production has set a "code" of perception and reception', from
realism to Indian folk theatre to English farce to Italian *commedia
dell'arte*. The issue of the powers of discourse here just cannot be
evaded: 'Language being one of the key purveyors of "tradition",
TARA ARTS was faced with the question of how it would confront
the text: a logical extension of the Company's desire to confront the
manner of presenting Gogol in Britain.' The rehearsal of the play had

to be 'as much about finding ways of "stretching" the classic text – of *confronting* the text – as it has been about "doing" the text'.

The play is now set in a fictitious small town in India just after Independence, and the 'way of seeing' the classic text is 'transformed' through the realignment of quotations, and the use of song, percussion and movement from folk forms. Addressing a variety of audiences about the connections between varieties of colonialism, external and internal, the production opens up a way of reflecting on relationships of power, 'In an effort, ultimately, to challenge received ways of seeing performance and reading texts'.

The second example concerns the uses made of psychology as narrative. In psychotherapy, issues of discourse have come to the fore in discussions of the nature of the 'self' and its relation to literary narratives. In recent issues of the *British Psychological Society Psychotherapy Section Newsletter* connections between post-structuralist literary theory and therapeutic practice have been repeatedly made by different writers. This work is mostly by critical psychologists from the Kellyan tradition of therapy. It is argued that readers of texts construct, and are constructed in, 'stories', and 'affect' is produced through narratives which shift the positions that a reader is called to identify with (Miall, 1990). In therapy 're-storying the past involves a struggle *between* narratives – between the stories that the patient brings to therapy and the ones the patient and the therapist begin to construct together' (Macmillan, 1989: 23).

Some therapists are going so far as to argue that psychology should become a 'discipline of discourse', because '[w]ords and structures in language shape us more than we shape them. We are vehicles for the conventions of language more often than we are achievers of something more unique' (Mair, 1989: 8). Again, this is not a simple academic suggestion, for the turn to discourse is having an impact even on the training of clinical psychologists. The 'objective' case study produced by the 'scientist-practitioner' is giving way to narrative approaches in which there is a form of writing which encourages reflection (Green, 1989). The construction of narratives takes place within relationships between trainee and professional and between therapist and client, and discourse contains accounts central to social relations, 'stories do, in fact, constitute the very substance of the whole human enterprise' (Salmon, 1989: 45).

In Australia connections have also been made, through developments in family therapy, with Foucauldian notions of discourse, in which the therapist has to take account of the 'stock of culturally available discourses that are considered appropriate and relevant to the expression or representation of particular aspects of experience' (White and Epston, 1989: 31). Relations of power/ knowledge pervade the therapeutic encounter, and the client is encouraged to 'externalise' the problem rather than treating it as their responsibility (with the attendant responsibility on the client's part to cure it with the truth obtained through professional help): 'Through this process of externalization, a person gains a reflexive perspective on their lives, and new options become available to them in challenging the "truths" that they experience as specifying of them and their relationships. This assists them to refuse the objectification or "thingification" of themselves and their bodies through knowledge' (*ibid.*: 33).

In different ways, both of these textual and narrative practices in these two examples are centrally concerned with empowerment. The slide from description to prescription in literary or psychological representations of action and experience is deconstructed, and new forms of subjectivity and social relations are called into life. It would be possible, tempting even, to take fright at this intensification of discursive self-reflection, and to conclude that the grand narratives of modern enlightenment thought are breaking down. There was always, though, a contested nature to the ideological systems of thought I drew out of my reading of Peacock, and the resistance to ideology was embedded in the text in its nature as a *satirical* text. Now the use of dramatic forms to draw attention to patterns of oppression in language and the use of therapeutic reflection to focus on patterns of repression in language are emancipatory accomplishments which must go beyond the frames of single academic disciplines.

The connections between literature and psychology throw into question the dominant explanations elaborated within each as a self-enclosed field of discovery and confirmation. Those who make the connections can no longer take the claims to truth in each seriously. They then worry about what happens to those who do, and they open up more space for this satirical work. The reflexive parody of ideological systems subverts them at the very moment it characterises them, and this then continues to provide spaces of power and resistance as necessary dilemmas of enlightenment thought. As an aspect of the maelstrom of modernity, this is a necessary part of the process of transforming and rewriting the received truths of academic and institutional power from the base up. This progressive impulse, the tension within modern discourses which makes the reproduction *and* transformation of social life possible, also makes the demystification of postmodern accounts of culture an urgent one. I turn to that problem next.

Chapter 4

Discourse discourse, postmodern psychology

> We were really shocked when we first saw the seeds. . . . We couldn't believe our eyes. Our insurance man was the first non-Muslim we showed it to and even he could match the writing ['Allah is everywhere'] . . . Allah is showing he is the creator of the world. I don't know why he chose an aubergine.
>
> *(Guardian*, 28 March 1990)

Political debates outside psychology often seem more depressed now than in the late 1960s and early 1970s at the highpoint of the 'crisis', and this has meant that the rhetoric of paradigm revolution and contests over theories and methods has softened somewhat. Things appear to have settled a bit, and, in the place of arguments over the ways in which the discipline has or has not participated in the oppression of ordinary people, we have milder debates over the conceptual value of attending to the accounts ordinary people give (Antaki, 1988). A symptom is that psychologists today are developing an interest in rhetoric, narrative, discourse. This does not mean that the turn to discourse is wrong. Far from it. The question is what that turn means, what else it carries in its wake.

I will situate the debates over discourse in this chapter in the context of theories of postmodernism, in particular the argument that we have moved into a postmodern condition of culture, from modernity into 'postmodernity'. I will set out two possible directions that the turn to discourse can take psychology in, then go on to show why the reflexive postmodern tendencies in recent discourse work should be supported, exacerbated, and arrive at a cautionary endnote about the role of critical psychology in postmodern (academic) culture. The future of critical psychology, postmodern or not, is intimately linked to the power of traditional psychology to absorb its opponents, and so it is worth reviewing the progress of alternative currents in the discipline so far first.

AFTER THE CRISIS

The dominant theme in the 1970s crisis critiques of the then dominant laboratory-experimental paradigm was a complaint about the positivist methods and assumptions which underpinned research on social behaviour (Harré and Secord, 1972). A 'new paradigm' informed by a realist philosophy of science was proposed, and the focus of research was to be the accounts people gave of their actions. One line of reasoning here was that accounts and actions had the same origin, and that the collection of accounts would be tapping the collective knowledge which constituted the social world, the 'expressive' sphere. In this way the trap of introspection would be avoided, for the object of study was to be shared social knowledge rather than private individual mental processes (e.g., Harré, 1979). A parallel tack was followed by those who drew upon hermeneutics, and they argued that accounts had the function of making sense as a *process* (rather than having, in finished form, 'made' sense). A researcher did not have privileged access to what was 'really' going on; a researcher made their own sense (e.g., Gauld and Shotter, 1977). It soon became clear to many psychologists that a key problem with traditional approaches was that they studied a silent world. Psychology needed to turn to accounts, to speech, to language. Although this trend was known as 'new social psychology', it actually affected many parts of the discipline of psychology as a whole, and still does (Harré, 1983; Harré *et al.*, 1985).

These moves reflected wider-ranging academic contests in other disciplines, and although the participants in the paradigm debates rarely refer to structuralism and post-structuralism, the 'crisis' literature was as informed by those conceptual developments as it was by the political upheavals in the academic institutions (Parker, 1989a). Academic psychology tends to trail miserably behind intellectual trends outside, and it was inevitable, perhaps, that it should only belatedly shift its attention to the organisation of language, to discourse. It should be noted that (i) the 'new social psychology', (ii) deconstructive attacks on texts and (iii) the analysis of discourse have been selectively and cautiously adopted, and

co-opted, by the discipline. It is worth briefly tracing the fate of each
of these three strands in turn.

New social psychology

New social psychologists (Harré and Secord, 1972; Gauld and
Shotter, 1977) have remained on the fringe of the discipline, and their
uses of structuralist and hermeneutic work had the effect of
marginalising them. Although mainstream social psychologists
recognised the value of the criticisms made of the bulk of trivial and
dehumanising laboratory work, there was never actually a 'paradigm
shift'. (This would in any case have been impossible as social
psychology has never been a natural science governed by 'paradigms'
in a Kuhnian sense.) Social psychologists could not see in new social
psychology the systematic methods for the prediction, control and
replication of behaviour they desire, and they could not take on board
complex theoretical debates from philosophy, sociology and
literature. They also suspected that some underlying political agenda,
or effects, would accompany the critiques. Since those times,
prominent new social psychologists have either regressed to the
mainstream, returned to the philosophy of science, retired or
retreated overseas. This stream of debate, however, did provide space
for other developments.

Deconstruction

Deconstruction emerged from structuralism as part of the post-
structuralist package of critical work on texts (e.g., Derrida, 1976,
1983), and a concern with taking apart texts of different kinds has
appeared in psychology in recent years. Some variants of this work
explicitly draw upon Derrida, deconstruction is used to tease apart
the dominant concepts in the discipline (e.g., Parker, 1988a; Sampson,
1989), and other attempts to make deconstruction more accessible
and politically useful to radicals in psychology have included a
number of critical perspectives on psychology's texts (Shotter and
Gergen, 1989; Parker and Shotter, 1990). It is harder to conceal deconstruction in the normal garb of psychology, and the signs are that the
mainstream practitioners will not wear it. They see woven into it
political critiques of the whole fabric of the discipline. Deconstruction and textual analysis are on the fringe. These metaphors end here.

However, the deconstructionist tendencies are useful not only in introducing the work of Derrida to psychologists and exploring the implications of that work for conceptions of 'the self' (e.g., Sampson, 1989). Deconstruction is one sign in the wave of post-structuralist writing which has mutated in recent years into what we now call postmodernism (Dews, 1987). It is also tactically useful as a way of disrupting theories, opening up *conflicts*. In the case of a critical psychology concerned with the dynamics of discourse, we need to open up conflicts, and not want to see them settled. If language and thought are inherently 'dilemmatic' as Billig *et al.* (1988) say, then to try to end disputes over the nature of psychology would be quite wrong.

Discourse analysis

Discourse analysis, on the other hand, has been successful in a short amount of time in marking out a fairly secure niche in the discipline. The current of discourse theory pursued in this book makes overt use of Foucault's (1972, 1980) descriptions of discourse and power and locates social psychology in the midst of discourses of surveillance and subjectivity (Parker, 1989b), and one influential strand employs Lacanian theory alongside Foucault's work (Henriques *et al.*, 1984; Hollway, 1989). The examples of discourse analysis which could be taken up by an increasing number of psychologists, however, are more careful about these Foucauldian filiations; Potter and Wetherell's (1987) work, for example, appeals to microsociology, analytic philosophy and, more cautiously, semiological traditions. Now while it is true that these traditions are, in some senses, as subversive as post-structuralism, and cannier traditional social psychologists recognise this, and that the representation and repertoire research has developed alongside more overt discussions of ideology (e.g., Billig *et al.*, 1988), discourse analysis has almost broken out of the margins of social psychology.

At the risk of seeming paranoidly suspicious of anything that is successful in the discipline, I do want to point out that there is a problem here. The success is double-edged. On the one hand, discourse analysis, in its description of the recurrently used words, phrases and linguistic devices which categorise and reproduce the social world, provides techniques which could build on content analysis up to higher levels of meaning, and these techniques *appear* to be systematic. The versions of discourse analysis tied to conversation analysis and sociolinguistics are most at risk here (e.g., Atkinson and Heritage, 1984; Brown and Yule, 1983; Stubbs, 1983). On the other hand, and this is the positive side, the versions pursued by discourse researchers in psychology have moved further away from this, and, although discourse analysis can play the scientistic language game of the discipline, it also breaks some important rules. It breaks the rules in three ways.

First, discourse analysis is deliberately reflexive about its own truth claims, and draws attention to the discursive construction of its own theoretical position and its 'data'. This invitation to reflexivity is not restricted to statements that any 'social text' can become an object of research and that the text of *Discourse and Social Psychology*, for example, 'should not be immune from this kind of examination' (Potter and Wetherell, 1987: 3). The inclusion of earlier drafts of their book in their book is designed to provide Potter and Wetherell with the opportunity to discuss their own activity as writers. This is not to say that they *always* succeed in including a reflection on their own position as researchers (Bowers, 1988), but they do struggle against the scientistic closure which afflicts much social psychology. Elsewhere, Potter (1988a) makes the point that discourse analysis should celebrate the ambiguity and undecidability of social scientific knowledge, and here the work appearing in psychology connects with sociological research and reflexive activities (Ashmore, 1989; Woolgar, 1988b).

Second, discourse analysis corrodes the truth claims of other supposedly scientific 'discoveries'. (I was being ironic when talking about 'discovering' discourses in the title of Chapter 1.) Many of the most useful examples in *Discourse and Social Psychology* concern the rhetorical devices that scientists use to support their own findings and to discredit the theories of their opponents. This line of attack applies to psychologists, and the readings that they make of one another's work (Potter, 1985, 1988b), and to the 'natural' scientists whose rhetoric is problematised by combining the sociology of scientific knowledge with discourse analysis (Potter and Mulkay, 1985). The relativism that results from this enterprise can facilitate an increased attention to what the knowledge *does*. Billig *et al.* (1988) also throw standard approaches to psychology (and our received academic wisdom about what individual psychology *is*) into question.

A third point is that the relativist and reflexive dynamic of discourse analysis impels psychology a step further into the crisis. Sometimes deliberately, and sometimes despite itself, discourse analysis breaks the rules by raising broader issues to do with the enterprise of psychology. Whilst the use of approaches to texts from other disciplines could serve to demarcate social psychology more rigidly from other human sciences, because discourse analysis demands a shift of *topic* from measured behaviour to the dynamics of meaning, it could also dissolve the boundaries. At some point the intensification of the crisis through the use of relativist notions and an insistence on reflexivity will lead to a choice between a political understanding of, a reflection on what psychology *does* (a concern with conflict) and a continuation of reflexivity as a solution in itself, an attempt to bring about consensus. I will return to this issue, but first I want to connect this turn to language with the supposed cultural shift in the West to postmodernity.

DISCOURSE AND THE POSTMODERN: TWO MOVES

Lyotard (1984) claims that the overarching 'metanarratives' of modern enlightenment culture have given way to the little stories of the postmodern condition. Lyotard's study, sub-titled 'a report on knowledge' was originally written for the Canadian government to help it assess how best to get into the information technology market. It turns out that Lyotard, an ex-Marxist, has succeeded in producing a desired cultural commodity, and features on the postmodern have sold avant-garde journals as fast as turtle merchandise. Not only that, and the Canadian government made a wise investment here, the moral of the story, or little stories, is that large-scale attempts to change society are out-of-date residues of the old modern age. The big theories of social progress and the scientific work which grounded these theories in truth are replaced by a multiplicity of language games.

In the place of modern political projects which traced the emergence of oppression and promised that collective action would see them end, we have pluralism. In place of truth, we have perpetual reflection on the impossibility of truth. Just as accounts of the social have lost their way in the postmodern, so have senses of individual identity. The personal meanings of each citizen of the modern state have given way to fragmented, contested and situation-dependent experiences which cannot be interpreted to reveal signs of the truth of the human condition. Humanism as a secularised modern translation of religious belief dissolves into the hedonism (or resignation on the part of disappointed ex-radicals) of the postmodern condition: 'intensity' instead of interpretation, or interpretation which will never kid itself that it has got closer to a true account.

What is significant about Lyotard's claims for discourse analysts is the reflection on the way in which narratives work as stories about the world. Discourse is now seen as responsible for having constituted a particular reality and subjectivity in modern times, and we are invited to believe that the shattered remains of discourse hold together the moves in language in the postmodern. There is no more than sets of competing discourses, and notions of social structure are themselves just discourses. This is a thorough, and deliberate, anti-realist world view.

One useful way to think about these transformations is actually to locate them in the context of theories of language, in the shift from structuralism to post-structuralism (Dews, 1987). While theories of discourse are reworking post-structuralist approaches inside psychology, outside the postmodern is a condition which operates as if post-structuralism was true. Postmodernism in psychology is the state of things that results when we come to believe that there really is no object of study but discourse, no way of studying it but discourse analysis, and no way of grounding a critical view of discourse but in reflexivity (that is, no way of grounding a critical view).

The relativism and reflexivity which discourse analysis prompts constitutes one more discipline in the social sciences as postmodern. There are two important ways in which the postmodern differs from the modern: (i) there is shift from a critical stance towards the world which attempts to realise human values and needs against existing institutions and patterns of culture to a positive stance which celebrates the way things are because any other way is as unreal; and (ii) there is a shift from metaphors of depth to the surface, so that instead of attempting to uncover deeper underlying structures of oppression, experience or progressive dynamics of change, the attention is to meaning alone. The turn to discourse is such that all there is in the world is seen as a discursive matter, and that is a good thing (or so we are told). In this sense, the postmodern is an experience of signification in which each and every thing is equally invested with meaning (Lash, 1988).

Outside psychology, this manifests itself either in deliberate references in popular culture media to postmodernism or in related fashions. In the 25 July 1990 issue of the pop-weekly *Smash Hits*, for example, the Soup Dragons talk about this: ' "We've been dabbling in Chaos Culture for about six months now," insists Sean, "I just love the idea of things that are made by human beings, like computers and mixing desks having a mind of their own" '(17). (The resurrection of Situationist ideas shorn of politics in some House pop or in the (uncredited) rehashes by Baudrillard are similar cases.) Inside psychology, the investment of things with meaning occurs in the context of discussions of discourse. Potter gives one striking account in the Calgary *DARG Newsletter*: 'The contribution by Malcolm Ashmore ... focussed on Latour's arguments about the actant status of doors ... and proposed that the appropriate Sociology of Scientific Knowledge [S.S.K.] approach was not conceptual critique but an analytic study of doors and their interaction with human beings. To this end he had brought along a fifteen minute video of doors filmed in various places on the Manchester Polytechnic campus' (1990: 11).

'Post'

However, to say that discourse analysis is postmodern is not to say that this particular expression of the claims of post-structuralists, over-determined in this particular case by microsociology, analytic philosophy and semiology, is part of postmodernity. We need to distinguish two manifestations of post-structuralism as it has mutated from a type of analysis into a way of seeing the world and of experiencing culture.

The term *'postmodernism'*, on the one hand, describes the conditions of uncertainty, frivolity, relativism and reflexivity in different artistic and scientific fields. These conditions are experienced as neither static – it *is* a state of flux, of *differance* writ large – nor necessarily progressive; in some cases these conditions are viewed as degenerate, and each area has its own point of collapse into the postmodern as well as a particular rhythm of adoption and resistance. It is difficult to generalise from one area to the other, though a symptom, paradoxically, of postmodernism is that one is continually impelled to try and do exactly that. In the case of psychology, the discipline insulated itself fairly successfully from other academic areas such as sociology, economics, philosophy or psychoanalysis up until the late 1960s, and did not entertain doubts about its serious mission to discover the truth about behaviour and apply it. Postmodern tendencies in psychology arrived late, and were unwelcome. (This partly accounts for their subversive feel.)

The term *'postmodernity'*, on the other hand, applies to the condition of culture which encloses and informs the abandonment of the grand narratives of humanised science, progress and individual meaning in all areas. It is sometimes useful to describe architecture, music or psychology as postmodern, and to use that term to fix a contemporary point conceptually in the process of acceleration of reflexivity which the enlightenment, modernity, set in motion (Berman, 1983). However, the notion of postmodernity is a little more double-edged. There is, strictly speaking, no such thing as postmodernity. There are, rather, pockets of contemporary culture in which it is possible to identify postmodern themes, and for which the postmodern condition may be 'true'. We have to take care to distinguish the collapse of the modern project in sectors of academic life and avant-garde culture from the delusional projections of that postmodern condition out onto the whole of society. Lyotard (1984) and critical writers, such as Jameson (1984), who engage with him on his ground are wrong to apply postmodern categories to the *whole* of culture. (Furthermore, the attribution of meaning to *everything* has long operated in religious systems outside the realm of the postmodern, as the quote at the beginning of this chapter illustrates.)

The distinction between postmodernism and postmodernity, and the correlative refusal to admit that *everything* is up for grabs, opens up a choice between two directions that a discipline like psychology could move in. Should psychology guard against the intrusion of the postmodern, prevent the prescriptions of postmodern writers from becoming, through the operation of a gigantic self-fulfilling prophecy, true, and try to understand the phenomenon of postmodernism? Or should psychology welcome postmodernism with open arms, dissolve itself into language, and lose its anchor in reality? This choice has been raised in other academic disciplines, such as sociology (Bauman, 1988a), but I will trace through an answer which is directed at psychology. The 'two moves' we could make are to use modern psychology to understand postmodernism *or* to make psychology itself postmodern. I will take each in turn.

Psychology as modern

The starting point of the first move is to accept that psychology as the science of mental life or of behaviour has been from the beginning a thoroughly modern discipline. Psychologists have been obsessed with trying to discover universal truths about mental processes, and have maintained a disarmingly naive faith in their steady accumulation of facts. In Britain this project is being accelerated as the British Psychological Society, with pretensions to become a version of the BMA, publishes a register of 'Chartered Psychologists' and aims to build up files of 'facts' which can be retrieved at the right time to be 'applied'.

We could generate a psychological programme of study of the postmodern, and perhaps this would both improve the discipline and add to our understanding. Within the array of traditional techniques are a number which could be brought to bear on this topic: (i) experimental and interview studies of attribution which focus on commitment to personal relationships, and the degree to which motives and desires are ascribed to the other (modern inter-pretation) or rated second to attractiveness (postmodern sensation); (ii) questionnaire studies which could tap attitudes to the modern and discover who is, and to what degree they have 'lost the nostalgia for the lost narrative' (Lyotard, 1984: 41), and whether there is a postmodern personality (correlated perhaps with Type B profile, external locus of control, paratelicism, etc.); or (iii) observational and multidimensional-scaling studies of the cognitive maps of subjects in the Bonaventure Hotel, say, which would (rather worryingly) lock into Jameson's (1984) proposals for a way out of the cultural logic of late capitalism. Maybe these are not entirely serious proposals, but there is a phenomenon of postmodernism at work in some way in some sectors of culture, and a decription of how it operates would be useful.

Qualitative psychology, and this would be the arena where discourse analysis could be helpful, adds to this some possibilities: (i) ethnographic interviewing, which focuses on the experience of the impact of information technology (connected with oral history projects to contextualise these changes) and the ways in which knowledge is used, could be connected with contemporary work and leisure practices; (ii) studies of the rhetoric and representations (employing hermeneutic methods) of scientific ideas and the ways in which these are turned into a 'common sense', and employed as true stories, urban legends or simple pragmatic language games; and (iii) participant research descriptions (using 'ethogenic' approaches) of the small social worlds and subcultures which are postmodern could be linked to work in the sociology of scientific knowledge and an attention to the academic interests served by postmodern notions (Bauman, 1988b).

The task in these examples would be a modern study of the postmodern phenomenon, and would usefully include an examination of the ways in which the postmodern has found its way into sectors of popular culture. I have a tea-towel, for example, from Australia with 'Foucault à Go Go' splashed over it in large letters and a text underneath the picture which reads 'She loved him in theory. But how could she find a place for him in practice'.

Psychology as postmodern

However, if the heralds of postmodernity are right, then modern studies of postmodernism are fated to fail, and to fold sooner or later into their objects of study. The second move we could make would flow from this view that we have to change psychology itself into a postmodern discipline. Apart from the quote (from Ken Gergen) in the publisher's blurb for *Discourse and Social Psychology* (Potter and Wetherell, 1987) which claims the book is a step toward postmodern psychology, a claim Potter and Wetherell do not themselves make, the term 'postmodernism' is slowly dribbling into psychology.

From new social psychology, Shotter (1987) cautiously uses the term to radicalise descriptions of accountability and selfhood. More enthusiastic advocates in psychology refer to the 'postmodernists' as combining constructivism and deconstruction and moving the discipline forward to give a more liberal understanding of gender differences (Hare-Mustin and Maracek, 1988). (Cf, Owens (1985) for a more thoroughly postmodern account of gender and Burman (1990a) for an appraisal of the problems this raises for feminists in psychology.) In sociology this astonishingly fast recuperation of postmodern writing has led to claims that social scientists could benefit from 'postmodernists'' attention to the value base of data, a point at which, we are told, 'postmodernists differ little from Weber' (Murphy, 1988: 606). (At any rate, if nothing else, the uptake of postmodernism, and it appears in this literature as a euphemism for a watered-down post-structuralism, could set up productive conflicts with the Hegelian fringe of the 1970s new psychology (Marková, 1982; Reason and Rowan, 1981)).)

It may be the case that postmodernism in social psychology will develop through the work of figures whose work was postmodern *avant la lettre*. Lyotard (1984) suggests some contenders for admission to the pragmatic and pluralist research world which has supposedly displaced the modern. It is instructive that the following three – Wittgenstein, Austin and Goffman – are both sources of the original 1970s turn to language and reference points for a cultural turn to the postmodern.

Lyotard's (1984) use of Wittgenstein, and in particular the notion of language games, is a first case. What is important to notice, however, and social psychologists would probably not normally notice it because Lyotard is following a move that the discipline plays with the strength of a repetition compulsion, is that the location of *conflict* is shifted. Conflict is not at the level of class or the State, but is to be found at an interpersonal level. The gloss on this is quite interesting. We are told that '[c]onsensus has become an outmoded and suspect value' (Lyotard, 1984: 66), and that the best way of coping with the breakdown of consensus is to recognise the 'hetero-morphous nature' of language games (*ibid.*). However, we are invited into a world in which consensus has broken at a small-scale level, precisely because (though Lyotard does not spell this out), consensus at a larger level is the necessary condition, the backdrop, for the little games to take place.

The use of Austin, and the meaning which is tacked on to the term 'performative', is also designed to have the same effect; it 'realizes the optimal performance' (Lyotard, 1984: 88) for an account of economic conditions which are now depicted as flowing happily and naturally from the activities of individuals. Discourses, now 'little narratives' rather than metanarratives, which mesh together culture are reproduced in a series of moves which redefine truth when and as is necessary. With this flows an account of legitimation which rests on the performance of the system, the system of moves ('paralogy' which includes, as a function of its operation, but cannot be reduced to, innovation). This, for Lyotard, is also now a description of postmodern science. This, in a sense, is where discourse analysis came in, for many of the examples so far of devices in discourse which have truth effects in the discourse literature are from the language games of scientists (e.g., Potter and Mulkay, 1985).

There is a danger that research into discourse will reinforce the view that the essential 'reality' of the discourse lies at an interpersonal level (though I have tried to prevent that from happening with an account in Chapter 2 of the way a realist framework looks to wider and deeper structures of power). Discourse analysis participates, then, in this series of games whether it likes it or not, and implies a discourse user who is either ignorant of the moves or, more often, is restricting their concerns to the pragmatic aspects of encounters. Lyotard (1984) is preoccupied with pragmatics and the ploys and moves which hold social life together. In many passages of *The Postmodern Condition*, and, not surprisingly, alongside Wittgenstein and Austin, Lyotard cites the work of Goffman.

Goffman (1968, 1971) provides accounts of the self-presentational tricks and turns by which we 'bring off' a part or role. The most influential strand in the 'new' social psychology, Harré's (1979) ethogenics, borrowed Goffman from across the disciplinary border, from sociological social psychology, and claimed to provide a theory and method in psychological social psychology to underpin Goffman's dramaturgical descriptions. Although Harré's ethogenic psychology was supposed to be rooted in a 'realist' scientific tradition, it tends to fold into an idealist position, one in which meaning overrides material structures of domination. Psychology should be concerned, Harré has said, with the 'interplay between a practical order, concerned with the production of the means of life, and an expressive order concerned with honour and reputation' (Harré, 1979: 4). He has claimed that, whilst Marxism developed an appropriate description of the practical order, it was Veblen (1899) who successfully described the codes which held the expressive realm together.

The fateful slip into linguistic relativism occurs when the distinction (a useful one) is used to make claims about the priority that should be given to (new) social psychology: for '[o]nly in exceptional circumstances does the practical dominate social life' (Harré, 1979: 35). This dynamic is continued when it is asserted that not only is the expressive sphere dominant in most places at most times, but that '[i]mpression management and other forms of expressive work involve control of personal style and monitoring of performance that calls for a higher order cognitive functioning than the consciousness required for skilled labour' (Harré, 1979: 31). This is a revealing claim, for the value attributed to 'control', 'monitoring' and higher order 'cognitive functioning' reveals the hold of *modern* conceptions of individual rationality and subjectivity. The problem here is that it is a modern conception of the person and its internal mental processes which splits the individual from the social and so falls hostage to cognitivism (a reductionist style of explanation that I try to counter in Part III of this book). Paradoxically, alongside the postmodern drift to relativism runs a modern view of the individual.

Not only are we invited to buy Goffman's dramaturgical descriptions of self-presentation (1971) and his account of the moral careers, for example, of asylum inmates (1968), but we are also drawn into the moral universe that his role-players inhabit. In this respect MacIntyre is quite right to say that Goffman's books 'presuppose a moral philosophy' (1981: 110), and that the dramaturgical view of social life is of a piece with the 'emotivism' of contemporary society, a moral relativism in which ethical judgements become reduced to individual preference, and which 'entails the obliteration of any genuine distinction between manipulative and non-manipulative social relations' (MacIntyre, 1971: 21). The bleak vision MacIntyre presents of the new 'dark ages' which have come upon us, where we have indeed lost the moral narratives necessary to an ethical human community, ties together in a disturbing way the microsociology presented by Goffman and the politics of the postmodern.

POSTMODERNITY AND REFLEXIVITY

This is a good point to stop and ask whether we should opt for the first direction I signalled earlier on in which we use psychology as a modern discipline to understand postmodernism or whether we should support the tendency of psychology to break with its past and become postmodern. This is a good point to stop and ask that question because a consideration of Goffman's place in the postmodern raises explicitly political problems, and it is a political understanding of the issue that is required. This would be politics in an unashamedly modern sense, and of a kind that is aware of the importance of conflict, in at least three senses of the word. First of all, it would appreciate the role of conflict between the liberatory aspirations of modern thought on the one hand and the conservative nature of modern *institutions* on the other. Second, it would also need to be a politics which opened up the conflict between reflexivity which merely dissolves our experiences in a plurality of different perspectives and *reflection* which grounds our activities in a wider context. Third, it would attend to the conflict between individual experience and social structures.

It is the third of these conflicts that I want to focus on, for it is salutory to point out that traditional social psychology, which we could expect to provide at least the attempt to understand the relationship between the individual and the social, is founded on the premiss that the gulf between the individual and the social can be bridged. The paradox is that while social psychology is supposed to be that bridge, it is not. Because of the way social psychology was formed at the beginning of the century in America as an experimental discipline trying to screen out the social as pathological (Parker, 1989a), it has actually functioned *as* the gap itself. Now the problem that faces radicals in the discipline is that the 'discourse' discourse resolves, or *appears* to resolve it. It appears to bridge the gap but it fails, like traditional social psychology, with dire consequences for a wider understanding of the reproduction and transformation of social structures outside discourse. I will show how by contrasting two ways of connecting the individual and the social. First, through practice.

Connecting: through practice

Outside psychology, it has always, in modern culture, been possible to bridge the gulf between the individual and the social. The connection between individual singular experience and general social structures is made through political practice. You cannot start constructing a critique of psychology without raising the question of politics, and, as the assessment of Goffman and the postmodern attests, the same applies to social psychology. The words 'critical', 'radical' and 'progressive' are codewords. They take on meaning only when a connection is made between studies of the individual and a political understanding of the social. The debates in academic psychology are interesting, but they cannot provide a reference point for understanding what psychology *does*.

When psychologists have been radical, it has not been in terms of their theories but in terms of their own political practice. The use of political reference points outside also leads to an understanding of psychology as a problem, and the modern project of self-understanding, progress and social reconstruction can then be distinguished from the modern social scientific institutions. It is only then that we will be able to distinguish between the way we would like things to be and the way they actually are. The descriptions of social life and individual choice offered by postmodernism are very appealing, and we may want 'modernity', in the sense of it being an alienating experience of serial relentless progression and a chase after the 'new', to end (Anderson, 1984). Buying, often literally buying, into the promise of the end of modernity from the relatively privileged position of academics and social science researchers, however, can lead us into slipping into a celebration of a politically regressive abandonment of modern political projects. There is some truth, for example, in the argument that, as far as the destruction of progressive humanist aspirations are concerned, 'the goal is no longer truth but performativity, not reason but power. The CBI are in this sense spontaneous post-structuralists to a man' (Eagleton, 1985: 63). These points about the end of modernity lead us to an alternative (mistaken) way of connecting the individual and the social.

Connecting: through reflexivity

The reason why the role of discourse theory is at issue here, and why the fate of discourse analysis is so closely connected with postmodernism in psychology, is that there is a powerful ideological fantasy that the chasm between the individual and the social *is* being bridged today. The turn to discourse provokes the use of 'reflexivity' as a solution to the crisis that each critical social psychologist experiences when they carry out research. Reflexivity is advertised, in some accounts of the postmodern, as the central defining feature of this new state of things (Lawson, 1984), and some of the enthusiasts of the postmodern in the social sciences see in it a way of overcoming the gulf between the individual and the social; 'postmodernists', we are told, advocate an 'anti-dualist position' (Murphy, 1988: 603). Reflexivity *appears* to provide the answer. We turn around and reflect on ourselves and our language. Reflexivity is used to denote our deliberate awareness of our place in things and our difference from others. To reflect thoroughly enough on your activity as a researcher often unfortunately, is to problematise your own position as distanced observer, and then to dissolve any space between the topic and the resources you bring to bear upon it.

There is something odd going when the connection between the individual and the social is made in terms of 'reflexivity' instead of political practice. My caution is that we have to understand the political functions of that connection instead of heaving a sigh of relief because a connection has been made. Reflexivity is an attempt, well suited to the postmodern condition, to connect which is *depoliticised*. And it leaves traditional academic disciplines concerned with subjectivity, such as psychology, in their place. The new discourse about the nature of discourse and the analysis of discourse in psychology encourages practitioners to join the spiral of reflexivity.

CRITICAL DISTANCE

Jameson (1984) takes the notion of postmodernity too seriously, but is right when he insists that we need to construct some 'critical distance' between ourselves and the culture we inhabit, and which inhabits us. The prerequisite for that critical distance is that we mark a critical distance between ourselves and the stories psychology tells. When a connection between the individual and the social is made through political practice, that practice distances us from psychology. It should. One problem with the turn to discourse is that we could lose sight of how bad psychology actually is, and the oppressive ways in which it operates when it is not just theorising but also practising on people.

So, tactically and paradoxically, the move towards the postmodern in social psychology should be supported *because* it is right to defend a modern understanding of the world and modern political projects. Psychology is one modern institution which has little to offer radicals. The institution needs to be opened up, deconstructed so that the conflicts within it become clear, so clear that it is too much to bear. This does not mean, of course, that no elements of psychological theory are useful – there are always helpful spin-offs from harmful enterprises, like non-stick saucepans developed from military space research (and a psychology book which is as useful as a non-stick pan is a rare thing). Here the strand of critical work in deconstruction is useful, and it is possible to engage with discourse analysis by emphasising, and thereby increasing, the post-structuralist influences within it, as this book has done. (At this point, of course, we *should* be concerned above all with performativity, with what the effects of our intervention are.)

This means that the reflexive tendencies in psychology should be supported. While they disrupt the dehumanising truth claims that the discipline makes inside, *outside* critical discourse analytic psychologists can develop a realist, *grounded* understanding of social structures. When critical analysts study the dynamics of discourse, they do so by bringing in an historical account of the development of the power of discourses and accounts of the institutional and ideological repercussions of texts. Discourse analysis can be put to progressive uses, but only because we also hold to narratives about progress which are more important than psychology. In part, this is possible because discourse analysis is still on the margin. None of the Discourse Groups operates as an institution. The field is open for debate and the elaboration of critical approaches to meaning. This does not mean that discourse analysis could not become institutionalised, absorbed, recuperated. One of the lessons of the fast uptake of postmodern ideas and their role in the derogation of radical politics is that the development of an approach to discourse dynamics has to adopt auxiliary criteria (concerned with institutions, power and ideology) and take supplementary steps which cannot but entail a moral/political stance on the part of the researcher.

This does not mean, however, that the discipline should just be pulled down, as if we could pretend that there was no such thing as subjectivity and no good way to talk about it. The experience of individuality in modern culture is private, isolated and dehumanised, but the attempt to wish away that experience as if it rested on nothing, as if there was no material basis, no human nature, would be as bad as behaviourism or as bankrupt as the promises of the postmodernists. Discourse analysis provides a way of describing the moral/political character of personal action (no individual can 'escape' from culture), the social nature of subjectivity. But how do we describe the person as 'discourse user'? We can see discrete biological units like ourselves sharing discourse with us, so what vocabulary might be helpful to capture a sense of the social *and* of the individual? I suggest some answers to this question in Part III.

Part III

Individuals

Discourse research repeatedly begs the question: 'what is going on inside human beings when they use discourse?' We now need to consider the model of the person which flows from the framework. A consequence of the usual refusal to speculate about the nature of the individual discourse user is that analysts could be accused of some kind of behaviourism. A further consequence, and one which has often afflicted varieties of behaviourist 'black box' psychology in the past, is that a space is left open for cognitive, mechanistic conceptions of the individual. If, as is sometimes claimed by its supporters, the analysis of discourse lays the basis for a *non*-cognitive approach, what alternatives are available? This third part of the book considers two models.

Whilst cognitive psychology conceives of the person as a mechanism, and, when it becomes obsessed with the notion of internal representations, splits the individual from the social, an ecological view treats internal 'cognitive' operations as the exception rather than the rule. In Chapter 5 I discuss how the ecological work of Gibson could be developed to provide an account of the person as embedded in language, and as moving between different discourses insofar as each 'affords' possibilities for compliance, or resistance. Aside from questions of 'ecological validity', the ecological model raises questions about the value of different discursive niches for individuals and the groups they belong to.

Whilst traditional Freudian views could be compatible with cognitive models, the retranslations of Freud's original terminology open up a contrasting 'humanist' description of the relationship between the social world and the individual 'soul'. This then warrants the turn to language in structuralist, Lacanian and hermeneutic,

Habermasian theory. Both developments, discussed in Chapter 6, provide an account of the place of the self and a sense of individual subjectivity in discourse, and each provides a different perspective on the role of reflexivity and resistance in the 'real' world as well as in its various textual reproductions and transformations. Each offers to a study of discourse dynamics a socially embedded variety of psychodynamics.

Chapter 5

Power: an ecological model of text-life

> Thank God for our bobbies. Their image has been severely damaged recently. *But how many of the Guildford Four were driving ambulances in London yesterday?*
>
> (*Sun*, 24 October 1989)

Psychology is supposed to supply descriptions of individual action and experience. Development, personality and the nature of thought are topics we try to understand in everyday life, and upon which psychology should have something helpful to say. Unfortunately, often it does not. Sometimes psychology confirms common-sense pictures of people, us, as isolated competitive individuals 'thinking for ourselves'. Here it reproduces discourses of liberal individualism which hold together Western (post)modern culture. Sometimes the discipline clashes with common sense, and elaborates stories about complicated internal mechanisms guiding indvidual behaviour. Here the administered world which bears (down on) us is shrunk and located inside the head. Discourses of rationality and machine 'intelligence' are used to reproduce the 'subject' as an *object* of a peculiar type. The role of psychology is contradictory, but the contradictions between expert knowledge and lay understanding are wished away. Its models circulate in texts, only in texts, but we are told to read them as if they were real. The discipline has the power to operate within a 'psy-complex', but it disempowers those it studies.

In and against psychology, however, there are alternative traditions of work which describe behaviour and mental life as embedded in the world. These traditions are worth recovering. It is not a question of 'recuperating' them, absorbing them into radical discourse, for critical psychology is too weak to do that, but an

engagement with the radical fragments of the discipline should help
rebut the charge that discourse analysts have nothing to say about the
individual. Critical discourse-analytic psychology drawing on
alternative traditions, such as that to be found in the work of J.J.
Gibson, could interpret contradictions in 'thought' as expressions of
discourse dynamics. Such a critical psychology could describe the
circulation of individuals through texts, and their (human) nature as
forms of text-life. Critical Gibsonian psychology could focus on
power and resistance, empowerment, transformation.

Proposals in the ethogenic 'new paradigm' literature, that people
should be 'treated as if they were human beings' (Harré and Secord,
1972: 84) and that people should be seen as embedded in
relationships with others (Gauld and Shotter, 1977) often ran
alongside the employment of Gibson's (1966, 1979) ecological
account of direct perception. Gibson, particularly in his later
writings, was seen as emphasising the activity of the 'subject' (Harré
and Secord, 1972), and as providing an account of the person which
was non-cognitivist (Shotter, 1984). Recent critiques of cognitive
psychology have employed Gibsonian descriptions of the
relationship between the individual and others and the world
(Costall and Still, 1987). The most important respect, however, in
which the ecological model of the person differs from much
traditional psychology, and in which there are significant connections
between the new-paradigm accounts and discourse analysis, is in the
attention directed to the location of accounts and persons in and
suffused with language.

In this chapter I will explore the value of alternative ecological
descriptions of direct perception and the embeddedness of the
person in niches structured by specific arrays of meaning. First, I will
rehearse arguments in favour of a Gibsonian ecological approach to
perception as an alternative to cognitivist psychology and make some
connections between accounts of direct perception and language use.
This is the point at which discourse analysis comes into the picture. I
will then introduce as an example a piece of text and take up the
problem of dualism as it is reproduced in discourse. The next sections
raise some more general issues to do with relativism in radical
discourse-analytic psychology: in the third section I extend the
account of realism given in Chapter 2 and discuss the implications of
an ecological account for our understanding of the relationship
between discourse and reality; in the fourth, final section I deal with

the significance of these ideas for a critical psychology. I shall also be supplementing my use of ecological theory at points with deconstructionist views of meaning, with the post-structuralist theory employed throughout the rest of this book. First, then, some reasons why we should adopt an ecological account.

(ANTI-)COGNITIVISM

Cognitive psychology has been looked to to provide the answer to a problem that has preoccupied *social* psychologists for some time, and it is an even more attractive source of work for psychologists caught up in the impossible fantasy of constructing explanations of individual action which are not social. The problem is, what model of the person is presupposed by our descriptions of experience and social action? If we were to accept, for the sake of argument, that phenomena identified by psychology (such as cognitive dissonance, stereotyping and conformity) were 'true', what are the people like who do those things? This problem can be, must be, stretched further (and this then causes more difficulty for the mainstream in the discipline): first, what if cognitive dissonance, attribution theory, stereotyping, conformity, risky shift, minimal group phenomena, social representations and so on were *all* 'true' (which they all seem, on some occasions, to be); and, second, there was *more* than this going on in our 'subjects' (which there undoubtedly is); and, third, we had to include ourselves in this picture, talking and theorising about what we, as subjects, were doing? What model of the person should we then adopt?

Traditionally, there are two responses to the question which neatly complement one another. These responses are often implicit, taken for granted. On the one hand, sometimes the answer is left to common sense, and psychology, particularly social psychology here, simply leaves aside a residue after distilling out the particular processes it wants to describe (and that residue is the individual). Longstanding traditions of work on groups and 'pro-social' behaviour in north American social psychology (e.g., Deaux and Wrightsman, 1984) offer this answer to the question, as do more recent European attempts to develop a theory of 'social representations' (e.g., Farr and Moscovici, 1984; Parker, 1987a). The legacy of behaviourism informs this response, with an emphasis on situational determinants of action, and a reproduction of the paradoxical relationship between situationally inclined psychological social psychology and its individually biased neighbour, sociological social psychology (Farr, 1978).

On the other hand, sometimes the answer is provided by focusing on the individual as information, attribution or representation processor, and social phenomena are seen as a result of the meeting of these processors. The burgeoning cognitivism in north American psychology and social psychology informs this response (e.g., Fiske and Taylor, 1984), and in Europe a similar enthusiasm for cognitive explanations has affected even the social identity theory tradition (Michael, 1990). Both responses divide the individual from the social, and the result is a dualist account. We are presented with a focus either on the individual *or* the social, never a model of the person to account for both.

In cognitivist theory, the information in perceptual input is assumed to be so impoverished that 'representations' must be constructed inside the head which approximate to the 'real world'. Perception is necessarily non-veridical here, and an awareness of the world can be produced only by supplementing that information. The deficient flow of stimulation must then be ordered into perception (and a sense of place, position, social subjectivity) by integrating a set of isolated sequential samples of the real world. An *alternative* to this model could be found in the work of J.J. Gibson and his followers, an approach concerned with the 'direct perception' of the physical and, I will argue, the social world.

Ecological psychology

Ecological psychology draws attention to the way cognitivist psychology merely pushes the problem back a step so that the individual is still *divided* from a direct engagement with the social through the interposition of an imaginary mechanical apparatus constructed as a series of hypothetical constructs in psychological theories (Parker, 1987b). In contrast, for Gibson (1979), perceivers are directly and immediately in contact with the 'dimensions of information' available or 'afforded' them. The individual organism and the world s/he inhabits are described as if they were a single system. Gibson argues that '[the] state of the perceptual system is altered when it is attuned to information of a certain sort' (Gibson, 1979: 254), and that 'one does not need to have ideas about the environment in order to perceive it' (*ibid.*: 304). He attempts to avoid splitting the subject from the object of visual perception: 'Perceiving is an achievement of the individual, not an appearance in the theater of his [sic] consciousness ... there is no content of awareness independent of that of which one is aware' (ibid.: 239). His account is of the individual embedded in a system of relationships, relationships with the world and with others.

The static conception of the world which pervades much social psychological description, not to mention psychological research deliberately unconcerned with the social, is replaced by a sense of continual movement. This movement is thus seen as 'regular without being a chain of responses and is purposive without being controlled from within' (Gibson, 1979: 237). Each system of structural invariants in the optic array is understood dynamically as part of a pattern of transformational invariants. Within the systems of information which comprise the 'niches' we inhabit is the specification for what type of person(s) we can be. The process of information 'pick- up' could be thought of as one of 'resonance'. This is a process Gordon (1989) intriguingly likens to a radio receiving electromagnetic radiation.

While this analogy serves to highlight the impossibility of locating the particular single component picking up signals, and so the stupidity of much positivist work on information processing, it also raises issues about the way human beings *differ* from such mechanisms. Human beings acquire a structured subjectivity which is in a continual dynamic of transformation and renewal by virtue of their understanding and use of language. The debates over the status of language (as a variety of 'indirect perception') in Gibson's writings can only be briefly signalled here (e.g., Noble, 1987; Parker, 1988b), and, as will become clear, I shall be adopting the position that an ecological approach should view our use of language, of discourse as 'direct', as (at least potentially) unmediated. While our perception of discourse is direct, however, the conflicting positions afforded by different discourses continually obstruct a direct engagement with others.

Discourse

Discourse analysis helps provide a variety of psychology where the question 'what model of the person?' starts to make sense within a thoroughly social framework. Discourse analysis responds adequately to each of the questions posed above to do with the social nature of the individual in psychology (questions that the discipline traditionally fails to answer): first, discourse analysis posits a framework in which all of the processes discovered by psychologists so far are 'true' (by virtue of the fact that the processes become 'real' as they are spoken of and reproduced within language); and, second, the approach works with, rather than against, the unresolvable conflicts between different explanations and the contradictory accounts people give (by making a virtue of variability); and, third, it draws attention to its own way of describing the accounts it collects and attempts to provoke the researcher, the writer and the reader to interrogate their own presuppositions, their own discourses.

However, the model of the person as 'discourse user' threatens to become, by default, a *cognitivist* model. Readers of *Discourse and Social Psychology*, for example, are warned against approaches saddled with the 'weight of unformulated cognitive baggage' (Potter and Wetherell, 1987: 146) and told that a discourse approach to categorisation directs attention 'away from the cognitive processes assumed to be operating under people's skulls' (*ibid.*: 137), but they are also told that cognitive science has 'insights to offer' and, more seriously, that 'analysis and explanation can be carried out at a social psychological level which is coherently separable from the cognitive' (*ibid.*: 157). The suggestion that analysis of these two levels of experience should be 'coherently separable' flows from a particular model of social life. This model in psychology forms part of the dominant dualist conception of the relationship between the individual and the social in the disciplines of both psychology and sociology (Parker, 1987a, 1989a).

The argument that thought is irremediably rhetorical, public and accountable is a good defence against cognitivism (Billig, 1987; Billig *et al.*, 1988), and recent work in discourse analysis has developed this line (e.g., Potter and Edwards, 1990). The discourse-analytic texts which unwittingly warrant cognitivist work are signed by those who have since, in practice, done much to undermine it. Varieties of discourse analysis which use psychoanalysis (e.g., Hollway, 1989) fall prey to reductionism in other ways, a problem I take up in the next chapter. My starting point in this chapter is precisely that 'it is discourse analysis which offers a systematically *non-cognitive* social psychology' (Potter and Wetherell, 1987: 157), and that it is now necessary to specify the nature of the individual as discourse user. If such specification is left to another level separate from the social, discourse analysts will find themselves hostage to the deeply ideological individualism that attends cognitivist explanations (Sampson, 1981) and a mechanistic conception of mind that meshes with a hierarchical vision of the social (Bowers, 1990).

It has been argued by advocates of the 'new paradigm' in psychology influenced by hermeneutics and phenomenology that it should be possible to take Gibson's work as a 'descriptive vocabulary' which can be applied to other modes of perception (Shotter, 1984). It is possible to pick up this suggestion and follow it through so that the 'perception' of the discourse user is that of a reader of *texts*. I will take a small piece of text below to illustrate my argument. My reading of Gibson's texts brings the notion of direct perception into realms of social life that we usually experience as enigmatic or obscure. It is the structure of, and relationship between, discourses, each of which is directly perceived, that gives rise to the feeling that we are separate, alienated from things and their meanings. When this is borne in mind, the ecological model could then be extended to account for the role of language as a series of symbolic arrays in which the various discourses which comprise it each 'afford' possibilities for compliance and resistance, reproduction and transformation.

The Gibsonian argument is that our experience of the world cannot be reasonably understood as a sequence, or even accumulation, of separate discrete stimuli. An ecological account, then, has no need to resort to cognitivist notions of memory (Still, 1979). For ecological psychology 'there is no dividing line between the present and the past, between perceiving and remembering. . . . A perception, in fact, does not *have* an end. Perceiving goes on' (Gibson, 1979: 253). This point connnects with the work on collective remembering (Middleton and Edwards, 1990). In this work, 'the mind and memory are seen as extending beyond the "individual skin" to encompass both the cultural milieu and the "body politic"' (Cole, 1990: viii). Memory is a thoroughly discursive matter. Discourses permit and provoke the phenomena we call cognition, and which we learn, in contemporary Western culture, to funnel into single minds. This connection with discourse serves to emphasise a crucial quality of the transformational array and transformations of meaning, that of *difference*.

Difference

Deconstructionist views of discourse have also emphasised this quality of difference. The view expressed by supporters of direct perception, of 'the organism and its environment regarded as a single system' (Still, 1979: 152), captures the interconnectedness of subject and object. For Gibson 'Neither mentalism on the one hand nor conditioned-response behaviorism on the other is good enough. What psychology needs is the kind of thinking that is beginning to be attempted in what is loosely called systems theory' (Gibson, 1979: 2). However, *discourse* as the symbolic environment of human beings is marked by the quality of difference, a quality expressed in two ways. First, the discursive is digressive because, as Derrida (1973) points out, language is a system of differences in which a final meaning is always deferred. It is instructive to bring Derrida's meditations on meaning in here for he deconstructs traditional oppositions between nature and culture, between ecological views of biological niches and the discursively structured environments speaking subjects inhabit. The second way in which the quality of difference marks discourse is that discourses differ not only from each other (a characteristic which enables us to distinguish them) but also within themselves (a characteristic which makes analysis difficult). Items in discourse have dynamic and multiple meanings.

SPIRITS

At this point I want to introduce a piece of text – *'Spirits in the Material World'* – in order to trace through the argument that an ecological account of perception can provide the basis for a model of the person as discourse user. What niches does the statement 'Spirits in the Material World' inhabit, and what meanings does it evoke and reproduce? Already as a set of readers you may have started to fragment into those who do, and those who do not, already recognise the phrase, and cutting across those new constituencies will be various positions, stances towards the statement. At this point, social identity theorists would posit the existence of a cognitive apparatus which groups must employ in order to relate to the statement. In this case, however, such a differentiation is furnished solely by this context, the confluence of *these* meanings, and our identification of the existence of particular 'groups' of readers is only a rhetorical device. The identification of collections of 'groups' here (as in much social identity research) is *only* in the public, discursive realm (Griffin, 1989). I will, as a first step, mark out two audiences called into existence by the introduction of this piece of text.

For the first group, 'Spirits in the Material World' is recognised as a phrase in a Police song (and the second group should be told that *The Police* were a pop group). Part of the process of identifying and marking the phrase is to attach a reference to it (i.e., Sting, 1981). It then also becomes part of academic discourse. A flood of connotations also becomes available to both audiences (now both those who knew its source and those who did not). For some the phrase may be nostalgic, for some it is merely passé. Some will hear the phrase also in the context of an associated Police promotional video which carried scenes from the north of Ireland and which was banned by the BBC (or at least one of my informants has this memory, and I pass it on as part of the text for the moment). For the second group, 'Spirits in the Material World' may hold within it conceptions of minds and bodies in which 'Spirits' are conceptually distinct from and are 'in' the 'Material'. This reading, more philosophically inclined and available to the whole audience (because the 'mind–body' problem is part of the architecture of our academic world), could see the statement as an example of dualism, an example, perhaps, whose implications need to be discussed. I have to be tentative here in elaborating a range of meanings of the phrase for different audiences in different discourses. This, for fear of legislating the correct meaning. There are no correct meanings, only contested meanings which both adherents and critics of an ecological discourse-analytic psychology can engage with.

The multiple meanings of a statement can be considered with regard to occasions of use, and it is the reification of such occasions into collections of people with a particular reading, and then into groups holding a shared view, and then into cognitive schemata in the heads of the members of the groups which lures us into cognitivism. We can avoid this route by just considering discourses and occasions of use. One occasion, then, for reading 'Spirits in the Material World' could be as a dualist expression of the relationship between minds and bodies, and as an expression loaded with romantic yearnings to connect two alienated essences. As an item in the discourse of dualism, it makes available to us a vocabulary in which we talk about minds as 'objects' as if they were there. As objects of this discourse, a dominant discourse in Western culture, their 'thing' status disrupts attempts to talk about experience and reality as connected, integrated, dialectically interrelated, ecologically entwined.

In a sense, the Gibsonian 'account is merely an alternative *description*' (Still, 1979: 153). It is an account which must rest on criteria other than those favoured by positivist psychology. While the ecological account may resonate with a discourse-analytic perspective, it faces the insuperable problem of describing social action in a language which is structured by powerful dualist discourses. The fact that many individuals within psychology deliberately subscribe to such discourses is the least of our problems, for it is the language we speak itself which is loaded against us. The language game being played here in this chapter, which has been played before on millions of occasions, positions the advocate of an ecological discourse as providing a description of perception as the relationship between organism and environment. The problem that a critical account has every time it attempts to posit a relationship between two sides of the equation is that the dualist assumptions contained within discourse, and not only 'explicit' dualist discourse, have to be employed.

Even the argument in favour of an ecological account falls prey to the traditional oppositions by virtue of the requirement that I specify two separate sides of a relationship. It would be appropriate here to think of the immersion of the subjects of such a debate as players well versed, that is directly perceiving and responding to a discourse they know their way around in a social context in concert with others, and the echoes here with Wittgensteinian accounts are deliberate (Shotter, 1990a). There are also powerful resonances with post-structuralism.

Post-structuralism attends to the way that language contains the resources to recuperate alternative, ostensibly oppositional, assumptions about the nature of the world, and this is why deconstruction, as part of post-structuralism, works 'from within' the texts. It knows that it cannot get 'outside' them (Derrida, 1976). It is hardly surprising that deconstructionist writers, such as Derrida, absent themselves from these already loaded categories by declaring that there has never been any 'perception'. This provocative claim is also designed to disrupt 'the presupposition or the desire for an invariable identity of sense already present behind all the usages and regulating all the variations' (Derrida, 1982: 303). Because it is so difficult to debate within dualist discursive ground rules, challenges to cognitivist designs must be critical of most of the discipline they inhabit.

The phrase 'Spirits in the Material World' sets up a puzzle, then, that psychology has attempted to resolve by positing a cognitive apparatus between the individual and the world, and between stimulus and response. However, in the extended ecological account presented here there is the basis for an alternative description which allows us to consider the relationship between persons employing particular discourses, and our vantage point can both be within language and be critically reflective of the operation of discourses. Here, the reflexivity urged upon discourse analysts can be pursued *and* grounded. We can also develop an account in our own discourse of the role of 'the real' discourse user, and here I move onto an account of different experiences of the real that are compatible with an ecological and discourse account.

REAL BODIES

The immediate problem discourse analysts face as they radicalise the turn to language and immerse themselves in the devices through which texts accomplish the social construction of reality is that of relativism, and then idealism. The illusion, itself borne by increasingly powerful discourses in academic debate, that there is nothing outside language always threatens to spill over into some notion of spirits (souls, gods, essences) independent of the world. Such an illusion is nurtured, ready to spring to life in mystical, sometimes dangerous forms, in dualist discourse. I described the solution offered by a realist position in Chapter 2, and will explore that position further now.

There are two ways to make a realist approach work in critical psychology. The first is to interrogate the positivist methods employed by the discipline, to take due account of the mediation and transformation of the real in the 'transitive' realm which contains scientific knowledge, and to re-interpret the descriptions given by psychologists in order to divine which structures (with what 'powers') have a *real* existence, in an 'intransitive' realm. Writers inspired by the 'new-paradigm' debates in social psychology, such as Manicas and Secord (1983), have championed this view. However this position, taken on its own, can fall into the trap of re-describing, in new 'realist' terms, the very cognitive apparatuses that a discourse-analytic psychology promised to dissolve. The clear danger here for the anti-cognitivists is that a realist position can turn, ironically, into a series of rhetorical devices which buttress reductionism.

The second way that a realist position can be introduced is to present an account of the individual as a 'realist subject'. It is this second way that I will take up here. The Gibsonian ecological model provides just such an account, for here the person directly perceives the world, engages with physical and social material as real opportunities for (and constraints on) action. When deconstructed, the agency of the person is no longer seen as 'inside' seeking expression against an imperfectly known 'outside', but as the exercise of power (and resistance) realised moment to moment in movement through the world. Aspects of this movement are physical, practical, and here the biological structure of the person as organism resonates with material niches. Other aspects of this activity are symbolic, expressive, and here the individual moves through the world as a reader of texts. Collections of texts define symbolic arrays which are the cultural niches we inhabit, and discourse analysis traces the threads which run through those niches meshing them together into 'society'.

Three caveats

There are a number of implications for the conception of our place in the social world that would be entailed by such a view of the person. Whilst the ecological approach provides a non-cognitivist, and fully social, account of individual experience, the consequences of the model are not unproblematic, and could, in various ways, still lead us on circuitous routes to an anti-realist position which would complement rather than challenge cognitivism. I will note three unresolved issues, potentially unhelpful consequences of the ecological model which lead us astray from a realist stance, before returning to my example text.

First, care has to be taken to conceptualise the activities and experience of the discourse user temporally (in time) as well as spatially (in space), and here there are serious implications for the character of research into discursive niches. The danger is that the ecological account could be reduced to a 'role' model in which persons are assumed to be able to take each other's place and experience. This position has been stated in the ethogenic 'new-paradigm' literature as follows: 'although no two individuals can be in the same place at the same time, any individual can be in the same place, position or situation at different times' (Shotter, 1984: 93).

This vision of fixed positions requires a denial of personal history and experience (and of the different readings of texts available to gendered, classed and culturally located subjects of discourse).

The ecological niches that Gibson describes could certainly be understood in this static way. As material niches through which an individual organism moves, they are fairly permanent, and evolutionary changes respond to the needs of a species and its environment such that the two mesh. However, in some of the descriptions of direct perception that Gibson provides there are also clear debts to both a behaviourist and a *Gestalt* tradition, in which the relationship between learning and understanding is more fluid. In discursive niches, sets of texts which present the 'reader' with a characteristic symbolic array, this fluidity is accentuated. The ambiguities, shifts in meaning and power–knowledge relations in and between texts that deconstructionists call 'intertextuality' make a static view of positions and possibilities of choice untenable.

Second, the ecological account turned to discourse, and the recognition that it is not possible to tie meaning into a system (in which we are able to adopt discrete roles), itself needs to become reflexive. To do that now, however, requires the elaboration of moral/political positions. Its account of the relationship between language and the practical order has to be connected with its own account of how a discourse user engages with the world. In other words, the realist position (as a theory of epistemology) must be matched by an account of the the subject as realist (as a theory of ontology).

For example, the realist framework allows an analyst to distinguish different discourses which constitute 'the family' as an essential natural unit of society, and then to show how such discourses function to normalise heterosexual relationships and proscribe alternative living arrangements. To accomplish this, the analyst has to draw on other work on the structure of society and the coercive character of family life (e.g., Barrett and McIntosh, 1982). Here, the discourse analyst is working with a realist epistemology (a conception of where knowledge comes from), and grounds discourse in the real. This is one side of the equation. A properly reflexive *and* realist account would match this with an engagement with the political effects of familial discourse as dividing categories of person inside (comfortable, secure, trapped, miserable) and outside (lonely, homeless, free, politically sound). In some categories, it could be assumed, are those people who *use* the discourses, directly perceiving the meanings they afford, and in others are those who *study* the discourses, seeing them as strange. In feminist and qualitative work the relationship between the two categories of person is explored under the heading 'the position of the researcher'. In discourse analysis it has to be taken up and developed around the puzzle 'in what ways are these people like us, and why can they not see it as we do?' An account of direct perception able to sidestep cognitivist explanations is also an account which makes a direct connection between (ourselves as) subject and (others as) object of discourse analysis.

Third, an account has to be given of the difference between occasions in which the Gibsonian account holds and the (peculiar) circumstances in which some kind of cognitive account has to be called to supplement ecological descriptions. This issue is, at root, one of 'ecological validity'. Language itself should here not be seen as a 'representational artefact' which 'wrenches us from the ecological contexts of animal life' (Wartofsky, 1980: 150). (That would give a particular naturalist twist to the ecological account, a point I will return to below.) An ecological account helps us distinguish between 'natural' and unnatural occasions in which discourse is used. This is an appropriate point at which to return to the sample text.

Another occasion for reading 'Spirits in the Material World' is when students read the phrase to be tackled as a question requiring a three-hour answer in a finals examination (' "We are spirits in the material world" (Sting, 1981). Discuss'). Now, what the statement affords (and demands by way of an appropriate response), as part of the array which comprises desks, clocks, the felt compression of time and invigilators, is writing. It also comprises others, but here the others are as enclosed, constrained, isolated as individuals. (When such a statement *did* appear on a paper under these conditions the isolation was disrupted briefly by a shared, audible and thus reciprocated recognition of the intrusion of an item from popular culture into an academic frame, but the enforced silence of the examination hall soon closed around the readers.)

In contrast to the previous occasion, and as a peculiar condition of memory display similar to the tightly controlled studies on memory and perception in laboratory-experimental psychology, an ecological approach runs up against some limits to its domain of explanation. 'The experimental psychologist should realize that he cannot truly *control* the perception of an observer, for the reason that it is not caused by stimuli' (Gibson, 1979: 305). Laboratory experiments are precisely designed to prevent people from transforming the situation, and, like our examinees in the present example, they can merely react to, rather than change, imposed conditions: 'the psychological laboratory is the very microcosm of the Cartesian scheme' (Costall, 1984: 99). How people cope here is outside the scope of an ecological theory, and the bizarre separation of subject and object is materially reproduced in the spirit of dualist discourse.

This draws attention to two important aspects of the real (*and* the connections between them). First, there are 'natural', felt needs of human beings, and it is necessary to attempt to retrieve the values of humanism from the traditional functions of humanist discourse. Humanist discourse locates responsibility for action inside the individual, and anti-humanism tackles that position for moral/ political reasons. Anti-humanists, as Eagleton (1983), a literary theorist critically employing post-structuralist ideas, points out, are concerned with the effects of material and discursive constraints on action and subjectivity; they are not people who refuse to give sweets to children. A form of humanism rooted in biological needs, demands and desires is necessary also to counter the temptation to assume that a simple turn to language can free us from all material constraints (and involves a necessary repudiation of the dubious history and effects of humanism). There is a sense, as Eagleton again points out, in which post-structuralist ideas evoke a 'liberalism without a subject' (Eagleton, 1981: 107). This view emerges when discourse is completely disconnected from the real in forms of relativism.

Language is rooted in physical and biological matter (as waves of sound, physical inscriptions on a page, vibrations within an ear, etc.). The second aspect of material reality lies in the ways in which persons as biological units are located physically in space, and it is important here not to lose sight of physical aspects of coercion. One only has to look at Foucault's (1977) descriptions of prisons and discourses of punishment to see that rhetoric is framed by and reproduces the practical order. Foucault makes some intriguing connections between discourse, power and an ecological view of subjectivity:

> power relations can materially penetrate the body in depth, without depending on the mediation of the subject's own repre- sentations. If power takes hold on the body, this isn't through its having first to be interiorised in people's consciousness.
>
> (Foucault, 1980: 186)

INSTITUTIONS, SOULS AND POLITICAL DYNAMICS

There is an intimate connection between power and institutions, and it is when discourses become embedded in *institutions* that they have the power to wrench our language away from its connection with our needs. Then they create a disjunction with reality such that (as in the examination example) the subject is alienated, and a cognitivist account becomes applicable. There are clear connections with historical accounts of cognitivist de-skilling of subjects in psychology here (Shotter, 1987). Here again we have to step back and ensure that we have an account of reality as well as rhetoric so that a critical psychology sensitive to the powers of discourse can move forward.

A third occasion for reading 'Spirits in the Material World' is as an example of a piece of text, and here I want to remind you of the political connotations the words acquired when the associated video was banned. Or, rather, to note that the images (of the north of Ireland) which provoked the ban connect a new range of already constituted associations to the phrase. I could, in this vein, suggest links to reinforce a tenuous, but sufficient, connection between the statement and the politics which looms over it. As a description of the power of institutions, and the peculiar isolated confessional sense of self which is produced within them, Foucault's (1977) history of discipline and modern connects the material organisation and regulation of bodies with the meanings we attribute, in discourses, to our positions. The power produced in the modern prison, for example, had 'a double effect: a "soul" to be known and a subjection to be maintained' (Foucault, 1977: 295).

Among the trains of association that 'Spirits in the Material World' connects with here is the importance of the materiality of, for example, the imprisonment of the Guildford Four and the Birmingham Six (Irishmen framed for planting bombs in England), and the destruction of something we call spirit or mind as part of 'the material' after the prolonged major tranquilliser medication many prisoners receive, which leads to (permanent) tardive dyskinesia. The modern prison, and its parallel forms of surveillance in the rest of society, produces a particular form of individual subjectivity (of a piece with that predicted and controlled in laboratory experimentation). At the same time, components of the *physical* techniques it employs destroy the physiological basis for the expression of that individuality. Here also is a disturbing illustration of the materiality of one area of psychological practice (Carlen, 1986).

The impact of physical techniques (and not only in the above example) does not alter 'cognitions', but destroys either the material basis for the expression of human needs (the character of the biological organism) or the circumstances in which needs can be described (the conditions for the employment of particular discourses) or both. The types of connection we make between the material and the discursive, then, do not require a cognitive apparatus to mediate between the two.

A point supporters of a direct perception account often have to repeat is that an ecological account does not argue that *nothing* ever goes on inside the head as an aid to interpretation and action, but it deconstructs the cognitivist dogma, 'the presumption that all psychological explanation must be framed in terms of internal, mental representations, and processes (or rules) by which these representations are manipulated and transformed' (Costall and Still, 1987: 2). The connection between discourse analysis and ecological psychology does not only provide a model of discourse user (a benefit to discourse theory) but also helps answer some problems that have beset accounts of 'direct' perception. Three issues that arise in criticisms of Gibson's work can be addressed once discourse is added to the picture.

First, there has been a curious puzzle set up in debates within ecological literature over the way in which an organism has 'direct perception' of affordances (as meanings) as well as physical properties of the world, and this has led some writers to argue that Gibson was therefore a relativist rather than a realist (Katz, 1987). Once niches are understood as being discursive as well as material, the false opposition between 'realism' and 'relativism' disappears, for we are able to distinguish different senses of the real in which the person is immersed. Second, the introduction of language into the equation also provides a point of connection between ecological descriptions and those who are critical of Gibson precisely because they wish to emphasise the materiality of signification (e.g., Sinha, 1988).

A third issue which can be addressed also connects the first and second points, and this is where we acknowledge the role 'cognitive' processes sometimes play in social action. The ecological account is, in contradistinction to a cognitivist account, not one which immediately, in its very language, dehumanises the person. Rather, when connected to discourse theory, it is an account of the conditions in which a person becomes dehumanised. It is, by this token, doubly reflexive, for it not only traces the emergence of the cognitivist discourse and the power that discourse has in the alienating institutions that make 'cognition' necessary (and cognitive psychology a self-fulfilling account). It also attends to the ways in which cognitivist rhetorical devices (which locate thought inside individual heads as a matter of necessity) affect its own language. Much of ecological psychology is a self-consciously alternative *description* designed to defend an image of the person as potentially directly connected to others. The location of that model of the person in discourse has, then, moral/political consequences.

Turning to an understanding of real relations of power entails an historical analysis of particular discourses, and it is necessary, as will have been clear over the preceding pages, that I use decon-structionist views of language to bring discourse analysis into a fruitful connection with ecological theory. As well as an analysis of the way in which language organised into discourse constrains meaning, the ecological model alerts us to points of resistance. The ecological account found in descriptions of direct perception resonates with a politics which takes ecological matters seriously, but need not do so in a way which romanticises nature and appeals to a 'deep ecology' as the touchstone of the real (Sylvan, 1985a, 1985b). By locating the problem in, and describing the separation of the person from a symbolic array which directly affords her or him movement and meaning as an issue to do with *institutions*, we can develop a sense of mediation which is outside, not only inside the head. A direct-perception position is one that sees that information about patterns of light 'is not the kind of information that is transmitted over a channel. There is no sender outside the head and no receiver inside the head' (Gibson, 1979: 64). When we see that 'information' conveyed by language is not sent from head to head but present in symbolic arrays, we arrive at exactly the position argued by discourse analysts.

Ecological psychologists have argued against the view that representations are manipulated and transformed inside the head, but this does not mean that the meanings we assign to the real, whether that is the realm of biology or of institutions, cannot be transformed. Action is not unmediated, but necessarily shared with others, and is structured through discourses and institutions rather than internal representations and cognitions. It is the focus on those discourses, the conditions for their rhetoric, and institutions, their real power, that makes a critical discourse-sensitive psychology possible.

Ecological psychology provides the kind of *description* of the activities of individuals as discourse users which could operate as a general covering cross-cultural account *and* it can account for the way in which particular culturally specific forms of psychology become embedded in what we now call 'minds'. It would be theoretically conceivable, for example, both for the Gibsonian story to be true, and for the cognitivist discourse to become 'true' insofar as it is lived in the action, experience and self-understanding of a population. This, in present political arrangements, is possible, and that is all the more reason to challenge cognitivist discourse inside psychology now. It is also entirely possible for the forms of text-life that a discourse-analytic ecological psychology describes to imbibe psychoanalytic discourse, and that variety of self-talk and subjectivity could become 'true'. This has already happened to an extent in the dominant cultures of the West, and different political dynamics flow from psychodynamic models of the person. The following chapter explores these models.

Chapter 6

Desire: psychodynamic models

> The new Tory minister for women ... was paid the ultimate
> compliment [at the party conference] by the chairman Dame
> Margaret Fry, after she opened the conference with a keynote
> speech on the family. 'Thank you for a wonderful speech,
> Angela ... and thank you most of all for being so normal.'
>
> (*Guardian*, 10 October 1990)

Traditional academic psychology keeps its distance from Freud, but
the turn to discourse and reflexivity now allows a reconsideration of
psychoanalytic theory. Psychoanalytic concepts circulate freely
through the discourses of twentieth-century Western culture, and
this also has a bearing on the appeal of Freud's work to radical
psychologists. The exclusion of psychoanalysis by academic
psychologists (and its relegation by them to the spheres of quackery
and mistaken common sense), and the diffusion of ideas and practices
from the orthodox psychoanalytic training institutes (into psychodynamic therapy, counselling and art-house cultural theory) has also
made it increasingly accessible, and attractive.

Psychoanalysis intermeshes in a peculiar way with common sense.
It simultaneously offers a vocabulary to non-psychologists which
allows them to explore and reflect upon emotions and relationships
without being disempowered by experts in the psy-complex *and* it
operates as a way of talking about repression and the unconscious
which draws the speaker into the peculiarly vicious spiral of
confessional reflexivity which is such a crucial part of the psy-
complex. Psychoanalytic and therapeutic discourses thread their way
through culture, capturing people in a variety of subject positions
and providing models of the individual, models which work.

In this chapter I will explore recent psychoanalytic accounts of reflexivity, and describe Habermas's and Lacan's discussions of reflexive psychodynamics before turning to the study of discourse dynamics. I will show how the development of a discourse-analytic and reflexive form of psychology calls for psychoanalytic theory, and how such theory throws light on the vexed question of when and where reflexivity may be appropriate or useful.

An attention to language and reflexivity poses a question to psychoanalysis: 'how does psychoanalysis employ the notion of reflexivity?' This is the key to an understanding of psychodynamic psychology (and social psychology), for the answers psychoanalysis can give illuminate the point of connection between the individual and the social, and provide a model of the person which *is* that point of connection. Reflexivity is a crucial characteristic of human action and agency, and the connection between action, agency and understanding is one which runs through psychoanalytic accounts.

PSYCHOANALYSIS: TWO POSITIONS

Within psychology, psychoanalysis is portrayed as an archetypal non-science so effectively that even sympathetic accounts within the positivist tradition (e.g., Kline, 1984) fail to challenge the positivist procedures used to damn it. It is only recently that alternative accounts addressed to an academic psychology audience (e.g., Frosh, 1987, 1989b) have broken from the systematic misrepresentations of Freud in textbooks (Richards, 1989). The caricatured psychoanalytic model of the person in psychology portrays it as being fundamentally asocial, or even anti-social.

The revival of psychoanalytic ideas in psychology has been helped by the debates over the (mis)translations of the *Standard Edition* (Freud, 1953–74) which render Freud's complex and allusive writing into statements of 'fact' (Timms and Segal, 1988), and by Bettelheim's (1986) argument that Freud was working in a cultural tradition in which it was clear that psychoanalysis should not be treated as a natural science subject to experimental verification or falsification, but one of the *human sciences* which appeals to the criteria of interpretation, experiential resonance and understanding. While Bettelheim's claims are debated (e.g., Grünbaum, 1984), they do open up a series of questions that psychology had long thought closed.

Psychoanalysis and Freud's work for that matter are not single closed systems of theory. There is no final state model. Two key concepts, however, can be briefly sketched out. One is that of the unconscious. Freud (1925) describes in one short paper, for example, a children's toy, the 'mystic writing pad' which consists of a celluloid layer (a 'protective shield'), a layer of waxed paper (perception/ consciousness) and a wax slab (the unconscious). An impression which we make on the celluloid presses the paper onto the wax slab and we see the mark, but when we pull a slide across the pad (which breaks the connection between the paper and the wax) the image disappears. What the toy captures for Freud is the way that the writing flickers and passes away, the way a record of the impressions remains in the slab as it becomes ever the more a jumbled, distorted, compressed mass of memories, the way the pitted surface affects the character of the trace made when the paper touches it on later occasions, and the way that the wax is necessarily involved in every image. The unconscious is never absent from writing, language, discourse.

The unconscious is not an inert wax-like mass however, but is dynamic. Drives within the unconscious, forces on the border of the physiological and the psychical, animate the mind in the body (the body in the mind). A second key concept is that of infantile sexuality. Freud (1905) describes the infant as a being powered by sensual need, but takes pains (in a famous footnote) to distinguish between the oppositions 'active–passive', 'male–female' (as biological difference) and 'masculine–feminine' (as gender characteristics). The connections between male biology, masculinity and activity and those between the female body, femininity and passivity are cultural matters. Freud describes the way the infant as a 'polymorphously perverse' (obtaining sensual pleasure from many regions of the body) and 'constitutionally bisexual' (caring nothing for the sexual identity of the loved object giving pleasure) being is forced through a painful process of development to restrict the zones of pleasure to the genitals and to repress any desire which is not heterosexual. Again, the forces and powers which destroy our wider-ranging forms of desire as we move from infancy are cultural matters, relayed by direct coercion and discourse.

The turn to language, and the embedding of reflexivity in language as a conceptual solution to the crisis in traditional social psychology, is paralleled by developments in psychoanalytic theory since Freud. Both hermeneutic interpretations of psychoanalysis and structuralist readings, in turn, reflect a growing concern with language in Western academic life, a concern, indeed, which fuelled the 'new paradigm' (Parker, 1989a). These different traditions operate on different assumptions about meaning and experience, and have different implications for notions of reflexivity. Two traditions I am concerned with here are German and French developments. It is possible to draw some contrasts between the way in which the most prominent living representative of the second-generation Frankfurt school, Jürgen Habermas (1971), using hermeneutics, reads Freud, and Jacques Lacan's (1977) 'return to Freud'.

Habermas and hermeneutics

The German phenomenological stream of work is fairly close to what Bettelheim (1986) had in mind as a human science. The focus is on personal meaning, with interpretation conducted as a variety of hermeneutics, and insofar as its adherents criticise Freud it is for holding too strongly to a natural scientific framework. As the activity of the Frankfurt School testifies, there is strong concern with emancipation, a striving for freedom which is intimately connected with the freedom of others (Jay, 1973). Habermas (1971) develops a general argument about the importance of reflection which is then supported by an account of Freud's work. One gets a sense of the phenomenological presuppositions in Habermas's approach when one reads that the goal of analysis (and here he is *not* talking about psychoanalysis) should be a 'new reflected attitude [in which] the situation comes to consciousness in an undistorted manner, just as it is' (Habermas, 1971: 18), and that 'the pursuit of reflection knows itself as a moment of emancipation' (*ibid.*: 198).

When Habermas comes to discuss Freud and a 'psychoanalytic hermeneutics', his account of defence is of '*an operation that is carried out in and with language*' (Habermas, 1971: 241). (The English translation of his *Erkenntnis und Interesse* as *Knowledge and Human Interests* (re-)introduces the *Standard Edition* terms 'ego' instead of '*I*', 'id' instead of '*It*' and 'instinct' instead of '*drive*'.) The description Habermas provides of our attempt to hide from ourselves and from needs we cannot face captures key characteristics of his position: 'The text in which the ego understands itself in its situation is ... purged of representatives of the undesired instinctual demands: in other words, it is censored. The self's identity with this defended-against part of the psyche is denied; the latter is reified, for the ego, into a neuter, an id [it]' (Habermas, 1971: 240). As we understand the *act* of censorship, we also are able to understand that meanings driven into an unconscious state ('delinguisticised'), and turned into things (It), can be drawn back into discourse. This discourse may be the text which is a person's life history or one of many subjugated discourses which lie in the history of a culture. The production of these mutilations, distortions of the text, is within language, discourse, and Habermas's psychoanalytic hermeneutics is not concerned with 'the understanding of symbolic structures in general. Rather, *the act of understanding* to which it leads is *self-reflection*' (Habermas, 1971: 228).

Dilemmas

Within discourse analysis, the authors of *Ideological Dilemmas* (Billig *et al.*, 1988) dismiss Habermas all too briefly at the end of their book with a simple characterisation of him as an idealist attempting to specify 'ideal communication forms' (Billig *et al.*, 1988: 162). It is true that Habermas (1970) does presuppose the possibility of undistorted communication, and he describes the attempts of speakers to grasp towards an 'ideal speech situation' as an activity which makes it possible for us to grasp instances of power and oppression in language. However, it is because of, rather than despite, this that Billig *et al.* are close to a Habermasian standpoint. Three close connections between *Ideological Dilemmas* and Habermas's position can be identified before we turn to the possible limitations of the notion of reflexivity as used here.

First, there is an employment of hermeneutics which reads 'implicit meanings' in discourse. Such meanings are 'not hidden in the way Freudian theorists believe' (Billig, *et al.*, 1988: 23), but the descriptions of, for example, a racist unable to employ meanings 'within layers of meaning of language' (*ibid.*) are glossed as 'untrammelled racist obsessions' (*ibid.*: 118). Second, there is a concern with a view of rhetoric which does not attempt to posit a non-rhetorical truth (see also Billig, 1990a), in which it is the ability to employ contrary discourses which is portrayed as a necessary and healthy part of 'dilemmatic' thought: 'unashamed bigots refuse such balancing in order to live unambiguously within their bigotry' (*ibid.*: 144). It is the ability to engage in argumentation which allows thought. They must posit, as Habermas does, the existence of a 'set of general and unavoidable communicative presuppositions which a subject capable of speech and action must make every time he or she wishes to participate seriously in argumentation' (Habermas, 1985: 86). Third, like Habermas, they argue that it is enlightenment which both allows and inhibits the ability for thinking, for 'dilemmas', to flourish. The contradictions which the liberal discourse of equality, rights and responsibilities opens up both has a content with a 'dark side' (*ibid.*: 100), 'darker themes' (*ibid.*: 101), and provides an enlightened 'argumentative' character which is preferable to 'medieval darkness' (*ibid.*: 105). (I note these metaphors here, for they mark this text, as all texts, as one susceptible to a discourse analysis.)

There must, according to this text, always be 'counter-themes' present, albeit hidden in discourse, for it is part of the dynamic of thought that it is marked by contradiction. The very similarity between Habermas and the view that reflexivity is 'an understanding of the ways in which knowledge structures itself in relation to its own development (historical consciousnes), and a recognition of knowledge as a social force' (Billig *et al.*, 1988: 161), calls for the employment of a counter-theme in which the negative side of reflexivity is recognised. Psychoanalytic explanations are deliberately disavowed in this strand of discourse analysis, and it is possible ('an implicit meaning') that this is a recognition that there comes a point when 'knowledge as a social force' (which psychoanalysis often is) does not necessarily facilitate reflexivity. It is from this point that the writers move on to acknowledge that a discourse analysis should not be allowed to conceal the violent, non-discursive (Habermas might say 'delinguisticised'), aspects of human conflict.

Lacan and structuralism

The French structuralist (often later referred to as post-structuralist) school is one in which the symbolic architecture of human society is viewed as both necessary and pernicious. Understanding the components of the symbolic order, primarily the family, enables an explanation of, and accomplishes an (albeit reluctant) acquiescence to, the place of the individual (Turkle, 1979). Whilst Habermas develops a positive view of self-reflection then, as facilitating the interpretation of texts and thereby dissolving the various defence mechanisms which maintain repression, Lacan locates unconscious processes in language in a rather more disturbing way. The very 'I' which contemporary common sense tells us is the undivided centre and director of action is a fiction, 'an impossible mirage in linguistic forms' (Lacan, 1977: 23). This sounds as if it does not exist, but the force of Lacan's argument is, rather, that fictions are as important as the real where subjectivity is concerned. And this fiction *is* a powerful centre.

The role of language, and discourse as a set of rhetorical devices, is to facilitate the development of this 'I' as one of a human symbolic community of other 'I's. The relationship between ourselves and others is fraught because discourse makes contact possible *and* distances us from what it replaces, that to which it refers. There is not space here to explore Lacan's assertion that 'the symptom *is* a metaphor ... as desire *is* a metonymy' (Lacan, 1977: 175), but it does serve to drive home the way a Lacanian approach leaves little outside language. Communication is not viewed as the transfer of the intended meanings from speaker to listener, but as the production of meaning in which both speaker and listener get caught up (Easthope, 1990). So, Lacan (1977), employing structuralism, re-reads Freud, and offers a negative view of the way in which self-reflection operates to tie the individual even more firmly to relationships, defences and repression. For Lacan 'the ego represents the centre of all the *resistances*' (1977: 23), and so this ego, this 'I', cannot simultaneously reflect on *and* free itself from resistance. Like other post-structuralist writers then, 'Lacan is centrally concerned with the constraining and illusory features of conscious self-identity' (Dews, 1987: 234).

Contradictions

In the elaboration by Hollway (1989) of the *Changing the Subject* (Henriques *et al.*, 1984) position, a deliberately (linguistically interpreted) Lacanian account of the falling of signifiers to the status of signifieds is presented. This is supplemented with a (Kleinian-inspired) description of defence mechanisms, but the account of the defences is of them as constitutive of relationships: 'If we cease to view individuals as determining the boundaries around beliefs, positions or meanings and if we understand defence mechanisms as relational rather than intrapsychic, then it is possible to understand that multiple, potentially contradictory positions in discourses can be divided between people in a way which brings one or both of them advantages (as well as losses)' (Hollway, 1989: 72). A paradox, perhaps a necessary paradox, in this account is that the author is both present and absent in the account (Cf., Widdicombe, 1990).

There is an 'I' (in descriptions of diary entries and thesis extracts) and 'my' (in descriptions of method and analysis) in the text which invites debate. In this sense, the text is 'open'. But there is also an 'I' who knows what some of the interviewees were like, and is able to add comments about the effects of one character's childhood relation with her mother (e.g., why 'mothering "signifies" in such negative ways' for Beverly: 77) or another's similar behaviour in his other relationships (e.g., 'Will's anti-sexism': 68). This second 'I' is not so fully present as to allow debate over the position from which such interpretations were being offered. In this case, perhaps of necessity, there is a point of commentary in which the level of reflexivity is carefully guarded. There are a number of occasions in Hollway's (1989) text when the position of the author facilitates the introduction of knowledge about relationships, but does not prob-lematise the relationship between the author and that knowledge.

At one point, it is claimed that, while a Foucauldian description of discourse allows an understanding of power and change, it is necessary to add psychoanalytic accounts to bring in 'each person's uniqueness', and that this involves a guarantee that 'the content is put back into language' (Hollway, 1989: 84). It would seem from this, and here would be one theoretical conclusion of these arguments, that a reflection as to the content of accounts and into the nature of relationships maintained by the defences should be continually pursued, that such reflexivity was necessarily a good thing in and of itself. However, in practice, some relationships are left unexplored (and it would be difficult to reflect further than Hollway already does on past relationships). Feelings are admitted and employed only in so far as they will make clear certain processes and (gender) relationships. The issue here is not that this text, which uses Lacanian theory, does not engage in a thorough enough reflection on its own presuppositions. Although such a criticism could be made, this is actually the opposite of the point I am making here. Rather, it is precisely because this text manifests, in its reluctance to reflect fully on the position of the researcher and the content of her subjects' accounts, its character as a Lacanian-inspired study of language, contradiction and identity that it works. The question which

Hollway's work provokes us to reflect upon is what reflexivity is *for*. I will return to this point after comparing Habermas's and Lacan's accounts.

Similarities: language, reflection and truth

I will outline Habermas's and Lacan's contrasting assessments of the role of reflexivity in discourse here because of the very different implications the two accounts have for a discourse-analytic understanding of subjectivity, but first it is worth drawing attention to three similarities between the two writers.

First, both Habermas and Lacan view the accession to language as a positive achievement, and this is because language is organised as the symbolic medium of human communities. For Habermas (1970), it is the hope of undistorted communication which makes language possible, and his (critical) defence of modernity, enlightenment, is premissed on the rational *and* rhetorical debates which it opens up. Lacan is less positive about the possibility for 'true discourse', but, affected by a French (Durkheimian) sociological tradition which stresses the importance of community, he makes an (albeit implicit) contrast between secure identity in traditional communities and the modern individual who must 'oscillate between narcissistic rivalry and a correlative neurosis of self-punishment' (Dews, 1987: 236).

Second, both writers are concerned with the nature of truth. Habermas (1971) devotes a great deal of space in *Knowledge and Human Interests* to attacking Nietzschean perspectivism (in which the world comprises a multitude of incompatible accounts, some of which triumph through the exercise of will and coercion). The critical theory tradition to which Habermas adheres must presume the nature of truth in order for critique to be possible. Habermas's (1981) defence of the possibility of truth informs his attacks on post-structuralist (and, more recently, postmodernist) theories. It is important to note that, unlike other post-structuralist writers (such as Foucault and Lyotard), Lacan does not accept Nietzsche's grim account, preferring instead a (more Hegelian) view of consciousness as arising out of a dialectic of recognition. That recognition underpins the function of language to tell the truth, and speech reveals an individual's desire for truth (and others).

Third, both place a value on individual identity. This is evident in Habermas's description of distortions in communication, though his claims that perfect transparent understanding could be achieved are tempered by a recognition that there will always be an extent to which 'the ego necessarily deceives itself about its identity in the symbolic structures that it consciously produces' (Habermas, 1971: 227). Whilst fragmentation and disintegration are celebrated in various post-Lacanian writings (e.g., Deleuze and Guattari, 1977), for Lacan such phantasies are a consequence of the development of conscious self-identity. The unconscious is produced in the shutting away of what is other to the 'self': 'the phantasy of the fragmented body is itself an index of the strength of the ego' (Dews, 1987: 234). The denial of self-identity, of truth and of communication, then, would, for both Lacan and Habermas, lead to something approaching psychosis. While their perspectives on the effects of reflexivity can be constrasted, this has to be understood in the context of their acceptance of the necessity of some degree of conscious reflection.

INTERPRETATION AND REFLECTION

The contrasting descriptions of, and reflections upon, reflexivity discussed so far can be explored further by considering one sample piece of discourse. The phrase I want to consider is '*I don't know what came over me*', and I will also use 'interpretations' of this phrase below to draw links with current developments in discourse analysis. It is a phrase I have used, and which you may also have used. I have often been puzzled when I have spoken or heard it, and wondered what it might mean above and beyond, below and compressed within the bare words. It is interesting, in addition to the issues it raises about particular relationships between a speaker and listener, for the general problem of accounting for our use of discourses we dislike. When we speak, we are often 'spoken' by discourses, and positioned as subjects in ways we may often try to resist. Our personal relationship to language is tense, contradictory, ambiguous. This is one crucial aspect of discourse dynamics that a critical psychology should address.

The statement 'I don't know what came over me' can be deconstructed. As part of a discourse it may function to refuse responsibility for action. As a rhetorical device within a (specifically male) discourse which justifies sexual excess, for example, it would reproduce images of gender tied to activity and passivity. It would also be possible to situate this within psychoanalytic repertoires of not immediately explicable unconscious forces which have developed from popularised versions of Freud. Within the phrase allusions (to coming) can be located in particular repertoires of sexuality. The interrelationship of these meanings, these repertoires, can be explored, and the historical reasons why they connect could then be understood in terms of power. Such an understanding requires just the kind of reflection on the social conditions for the emergence of discourse that Habermas and (less explicitly) Lacan recommend. However, it is when we move into the fine grain of the phrase that the issue of reflexivity becomes more apparent.

In this single statement of eight words there are: (i) the evocation of immediately unaccountable feelings ('what came over', 'what' it was, with the uncomprehended 'it' as a resource which may be a mere accounting device or the placing of something which needs to be explored further, which is as yet 'Id'); (ii) the splitting of experience (such that the 'I' at the beginning of the statement is the 'I' that 'don't know' how it happened to an other, 'me', 'me' as object rather than the subject of events, but a 'me' who was once and will again be 'I'); and (iii) the appeal to an implicit temporally grounded excuse for, and moral comment on, action (in which the position of the 'I' as subject is metaphorically above the 'me', and is marked as a place from which to comment as an 'Above-I'). Did you check that the statement contained eight words?

The statement 'I don't know what came over me' has appeared twice so far, now three times, and then in parts, and each reading addresses you as reader in a different way. (Its repetition may also become an issue. Did you check that the statement contains eight words?) The reading of texts is crucial to discourse analysis, for discourses address subjects, they appeal to the attention of the reader in distinct intellectual and emotional modes. One traditional way of interpreting such texts (traditional in both psychology and in psychoanalysis) is to turn attention to the speaker of the text. 'I don't know what came over me' becomes a 'problem' to be investigated, and when the reasons an *individual* intended (consciously or unconsciously) it are discovered the puzzle is solved. In contrast, discourse analysis often finds itself with texts in which there are only readers (for it is often impossible to turn to the author to ask them what they meant). It is not possible to investigate the author of the text, and it would not necessarily help the (discourse) analyst to divine a speaker's/writer's intentions in order to locate the statement in a repertoire. Instead, we need to turn attention to our place in the text as it addresses us. The 'I' evoked *in* the text as it is read is what should concern us. It is your and my reaction, the way in which the text engages you and me as subjects which is important, for the connotations of the phrase will help us to locate it in broader systems of meaning which operate regardless of individual intention.

I have suggested some discourses in which the statement 'I don't know what came over me' could live, and some further thoughts on what is being said within it about the relationship between an 'I', 'me' and 'it'. It would, of course, be reductive to say that this *is* the interpretation, and leave it at that. We have to contextualise it. One of the problems with the traditional academic psychological textbook treatments of psychoanalysis is that the impression is given that it is possible to provide definitive interpretations regardless of context (Richards, 1989). As part of a human science, however, a variety of psychoanalysis which is applied to texts, and the discourses which inform those texts, can only offer plausible suggestions as to what may underly a text and what it may conceal. This is where the accounts Habermas and Lacan offer are useful, for they call for descriptions of the dynamics underlying discourse which are concerned with relationships, symbolically maintained relationships which contain particular distortions which have to be unravelled. Lacan leaves little outside language in his account, but just enough for language to produce an 'ego' experienced as real (Parker, in press). I now want to bring Habermasian and Lacanian readings to bear on the statement, readings which *require* a further specification of possible occasions in which the statement would be read/heard.

Interpretative contexts

I contrasted Habermas's and Lacan's conceptions of reflexivity, but not in order to arrive at a judgement as to which is correct and which mistaken. I will now outline some contexts for my sample statement, in order to support two suggestions about reflexivity. The first is that we need a judicious blend of the two notions of reflexivity, of (i) the way it is possible to reflect on discourse and (ii) what the effects of that reflection are. We can employ *both* notions of reflexivity, and it is useful to do so on different occasions. When and where we adopt the line that events and relationships are rendered usefully transparent through reflection or the argument that these matters would be obscured further by an attempt to reflect is a strategic decision. The second suggestion is that neither notion of reflexivity on offer is sufficient. We have to go beyond the accounts that people offer, or texts that we read, both to decide when to adopt a Habermasian- or Lacanian-inclined reading and to contextualise the things we are analysing. I will describe occasions on which a Habermasian view and sympathy for reflection may be of value and occasions on which a Lacanian reading more suspicious of the benefits of reflexivity would be appropriate.

First, consider the use of the phrase in the context of a political scandal, perhaps in the extreme case of an officer in a dictatorship explaining orders which led to deaths of dissidents. Another use might be by a union bureaucrat explaining his or her agreement with a disastrous wage and conditions agreement in a meeting with management. In these instances, the warrant 'I don't know what came over me' can be explored further, and the form and function of the phrase can be understood as being a *distortion* of a state of affairs. The phrase operates both to individualise the issue and to obscure what has been going on. We could say that we need to see things 'as they are'. Following Habermas, we could say that an understanding of how and why the phrase operates to justify murder or betrayal, and how and why the speaker has investments which are concealed by the use of the phrase, would be emancipatory.

But consider other occasions, perhaps in the context of someone excusing themselves eating a box of sweets which were a present for someone else. Another setting might be the attempt of a lover to placate their partner after saying something hurtful. Now, in these instances, the warrant 'I don't know what came over me' could be interrogated further, but it is perhaps more appropriate to adopt a Lacanian view of the way in which a reflection on the use of the statement re-positions the addressor and addressee in relation to one another. Perhaps, in the worst of scenarios, the attempt to reflect operates to intensify the problem because a double-bind has unwittingly been set up. At the very least, the statement represents what is happening, and the re-establishment of a relationship is accomplished by the fact that a warrant was offered, rather than what the *content* of the warrant was. The drive to reflect makes it impossible to accept attempts to repair a split with a simple 'I didn't mean to say (what I said)'. In some senses, of course, such a statement, any statement, could not be so simple, but what these occasions demonstrate is that there are times when 'reflexivity' itself becomes a problem rather than a solution. Discourse analysis advocates reflexivity because 'talk has the property of being both *about* actions, events and situations, and at the same time *part* of those things' (Potter and Wetherell, 1987: 182). Being 'part of' the action makes it impossible for the analyst to treat subjects as if they were objects, but it also calls for a different view of what 'subjects' are.

DILEMMAS, CONTRADICTIONS, DYNAMICS

The 'model' of the 'person' which critical psychology has been searching for but has so far been unable to find is one which conceives of subjectivity as *the point of contact* between the individual and the social (rather than opting for one or the other). The activity of reflection is crucial here, but not the key to something else. Two general issues follow from this: first, that it is appropriate on some occasions to refrain from reflection; and, second, that different texts may be read in different ways because of the way they are constructed. Just as there are different occasions in which certain analyses of 'I don't know what came over me' could be employed, so there are different research circumstances in which particular varieties of discourse analysis are appropriate. An underlying assumption here, of course, is that whatever variety of psychoanalysis we adopt, the vocabulary Freud developed allows us to reflect on our reactions to these texts, and on how the discourses they describe affect us.

One single notion of reflexivity is not sufficient, and a problem shared by Habermas and Lacan is that neither provides an adequate account of the relationship between language and 'the real'. For Habermas, the concern with the possibility of an 'ideal speech situation' is part of a conception of social structures and their amelioration in which it is the systematic distortions which are the problem rather than the interests they serve. For Lacan, 'the Real' (Habermas's 'outer nature') is 'impossible', always outside 'the Imaginary' (Habermas's 'inner nature') and 'the Symbolic' (roughly corresponding to Habermas's 'society') (Dews, 1987). Alternative formulations, a mite easier to accept, mark the distinction between what is possible and what is impossible to change: 'the opposite of the possible is certainly the real' (Lacan, 1979: 167).

In order to determine how to use the notion of reflexivity, we need other criteria. We need both a moral position (in which we are able to appreciate the role of accountability, rights to speak and desire) and a political position (in which we have an understanding of the wider circumstances in which the statements are made). A combination of these positions would amount to something approximating a critical realist view of discourse, social structures and experience. Reflexivity is a necessary but not a sufficient condition for an understanding of relationships and how they are reproduced in discourse, and it is not necessarily a step in the right direction when taken on its own. If it is employed as if it was the solution on its own, it may be worse than no help at all insofar as it fails to problematise power relations.

Two caveats to my argument are necessary here. First, it should be said that in these discourse approaches, there is an identifiable political motivation, with the authors' commitment to anti-racist politics (Potter and Wetherell, 1987; Billig *et al.*, 1988) and feminism (Hollway, 1989) clearly marking the content and presentation of these texts. (Another text, *The Politics of Mental Health* (Banton *et al.*, 1985), should also be mentioned here as employing Foucauldian styles of both discourse theory and psychoanalysis to develop a critical account of mental health practice. It has had some influence on the development of discourse work in psychology, and carefully uses a reflection on its own accounts as a way of problematising power relations.) The contradictions, and possible pitfalls I identify, are mitigated by a political stance in these cases. A problem is that as discourse analysis becomes more popular, is recuperated, it will be less likely that such checks will operate.

A second caveat is that these cases do, or could, employ psychoanalysis merely as a research tool. It is not possible to draw strict analogies between the analysis of a text and a psychoanalysis in which the person speaks back, and insofar as there is a therapeutic effect in this work it is secondary to the political effects of researching particular topics and empowering those who are studied and who read the accounts. In a therapeutic setting, the following of paths of description or reflection is judged, carefully chosen as the moment warrants, perhaps somewhat in the manner I have suggested it should be chosen in discourse analysis. The problems I identify are, again, problems that will attend the popularisation of a 'method' in psychology in which such moral/political judgements become less important than the drive to collect results.

In addition to the question 'what model of the person is

presupposed by discourse analysis?', and a second question 'what notion of reflexivity does psychoanalysis adopt?' (if it promises to provide the answer to the first question), we need to introduce a third question (which I have been addressing through the course of this book) which is to do with how we step back and offer a wider account which contextualises the activities of psychology, reflexivity and psychoanalysis. The solution is not simply to opt for one of the styles of discourse analysis, but to read them again with different notions of reflexivity in mind, to bring some psychoanalytic concepts to bear on these writers' discourse, and to assess how these concepts could play harmful and helpful roles.

These debates serve to emphasise that people cannot, as discourse analysts admit, have 'perfect insight' (Potter and Wetherell 1987: 177). These debates also serve to deconstruct, by the same token, the claim that discourse analysts who recognise the potentially reflexive nature of their work are 'simply more honest' (ibid.: 182). The recent developments inspired by post-structuralism, both in uses of the approach and in hermeneutic rebuttals, provide ways of thinking about the value of reflexivity, reflexivity that Habermas emphasises and the negative aspects of which concerned Lacan. An overall advantage is that the employment of psychoanalysis would serve to protect discourse analysis against a recuperation by 'scientific' behaviourist or cognitive theory, and bring it, without retreating into 'humanism', closer to developments outside psychology.

Dilemmas and contradictions

The choice of models of the individual in a discourse-analytic psychology carries with it a host of issues and complications, and the way I have posed the ecological and psychodynamic alternatives in these last two chapters has been to 'suspend disbelief' and sympathetically explore each of them. For an ecological psychologist, the speculations about internal cognitive states (and it is difficult not to treat the structural division of the mind into libidinally charged agencies, the operation of defence mechanisms, the account of the perception of relationships as marked by transference and so on as cognitive matters of some kind) make the psychodynamic model as unappealing as some of mainstream cognitivist psychology's pictures of the mind. For a psychodynamic writer, the ecological approach could be suspected of romanticising an unmediated contact between the individual and the world, and then between the individual and others. The phantasies of direct perception are no less dubious (and rooted inside the mind, and in infancy) than the cognitivist desire to predict and control.

The reflexive strands of discourse theory, in the sociology of science and then in the playful writings of some of those in the Discourse Groups, would want to problematise all such 'models': 'why fix the image of the person in this way?' In part, the opposition to models here is symptomatic of a deeper suspicion of any overarching theoretical framework (or 'metanarrative'). Those taken with rhetoric would question, quite rightly, the ways in which images of the individual and the social are used to bring off different effects. The rhetoric of ecology, for example, has resonances with friendly green attitudes and functions as an opposition to hard scientistic cognitive psychology. This makes opposition to it seem reactionary and bad-tempered. Psychoanalytic rhetoric plays the trick, of course, of constructing an opposition between traditional experimental psychology and psychodynamic varieties, and then discrediting opponents (and anyone else who demurs) by alluding to mechanisms of repression and defence. What the theories do is more important than what they are. The discourses of ecology and psychodynamics are bound up with overall representations of the world, and a focus on these representations could also highlight the way experimental practices have absorbed Gibsonian 'alternatives', and the way psychoanalytic practice allows some categories of person (merely) to speak and some to interpret. How we choose between models of the individual, then, is complicated by the rhetorical and representational issues discourse analysts address. These issues in turn bring us back out of the limited frame of these two chapters, back to the wider context explored in the three parts of this book.

Dynamics

The different discourse traditions focus on different aspects of the powers of language, but the texts they work on are embedded in relatively enduring structures of power and resistance. The vocabularies of ecological or psychodynamic psychology are also framed by cultures preoccupied with the nature of the individual. In some respects the argument traced through the course of the book is clear. I followed the line that Foucauldian work on language is a useful resource for discourse analysis, but that it is possible to employ criteria for the identification of discourses and that a realist account is necessary to contextualise those discourses. This means that we need to resist the view popular in postmodern accounts that there is nothing more important than language and the view popular in psychology that internal cognitions allow us to use discourse. In other respects, I have been less certain. I have wanted to argue that we should make discourse analysis say something about institutions, power and ideology, but that it is not intrinsic to the approach that it do that. I took up the claims that a postmodern state of culture is now in place, and argued that it was not (perhaps because I wished it was not). Now (in a manner disturbingly in keeping with the postmodern spirit), I have proposed models of the individual which are not revealed truths, but simply descriptions, vocabularies, repertoires. What is mistaken and what is correct about these different vocabularies will have to be developed in debates which are rooted in individual and discourse dynamics outside psychology.

Research and reading

> Imagine the shock, for a reader reared on the carefully sanitised pabulum of the proposed new liturgy, of stumbling across the strong meat of the unreconstructed Word.
>
> (Moore, 1989)

Research into discourse should be led by the issues and problems that are to be addressed and, where possible, by research participants (those called 'subjects' in traditional positivist psychology). Discourse analysis is not, or should not be, a 'method' to be wheeled on and applied to any and every topic. All of those inside and outside the existing Discourse Groups which focus on method are aware that they are taking the risk of making an analytic sensitivity to discourse become just another thoughtless empirical technique. These notes on references for discourse work cover (1) 'methods' in qualitative research and discourse, (2) empirical studies of discourse, (3) discourse-orientated critiques of other approaches in psychology, (4) other introductory texts and sources on the topics pursued by those using discourse analysis, (5) critical responses to discourse analysis, and (6) theoretical issues.

QUALITATIVE RESEARCH AND DISCOURSE

There are many types of text, and discourse analysis can be turned to different material, ranging from interviews to group discussions to newspaper articles to advertisements. The structure of a report on discourse could usefully follow a format in which there is: (i) an 'introduction', in which other work on the topic (from the traditional or discourse literature) is covered, in which the types of texts that will be studied are described, and in which questions (the nearest we get to hypotheses) about the construction, functions and variability of meaning (*à la* Potter and Wetherell, 1987) are raised; (ii) a 'methodology' section, in which the specific texts to be analysed are described together with how you collected (or chose) them, and here you could also say why certain texts were *not* used, and in which some details about transcription conventions (in the case of interviews, media recordings or discussions) or group discussion (particularly in the case of the analysis of visual material) are given; (iii) an 'analysis' section in which the coding of the material organises excerpts from the texts under the different discourse headings, together with some elaboration of the way they interrelate to give rise to certain tacit assumptions about roles, 'political' effects and social positions; and (iv) a discussion section in which the analysis is related to other material, and in which there is some reflection on the issues raised by the method including, crucially in the case of material in which you participated (such as interviews), the position of the researcher. In the following four sections I will draw attention to some of the issues that could be addressed under these report headings.

'Introduction'

The way that language plays a powerful role in reproducing and transforming power relations along many different dimensions (of class, culture, gender, sexuality, disability and age, etc.) is lucidly discussed by Andersen (1988). Most methods in psychology are simply unsuitable for exploring those issues. Because qualitative researchers are still in a minority in the discipline, empirical projects still have, each time, to rehearse the problems with positivist approaches, referring, for example, to Harré and Secord's (1972) critique of old-paradigm laboratory-experimental social psychology, and drawing, perhaps, on Reason and Rowan's (1981) extensive selection of alternative new-paradigm approaches and examples. (There is, for example, a good discussion of the way the grip of positivist methodology on research into psychotherapeutic provision in the National Health Service was tackled at thesis level by Pilgrim (1990).) This ground clearing will then need to lead on to an outline of the principles of discourse analysis (see the section on introductory texts and sources below). It might be useful to address stage one of Potter and Wetherell's (1987) 'ten stages in the analysis of discourse' here.

'Methodology'

If the material is to be obtained from interviews, a decision has to be made about the type of interviewing process to be adopted. Structured interviewing, in which there are pre-set categories, threatens, of course, to smother the very variability that discourse analysis celebrates. Semi-structured interviewing is preferable, and ethnographic interviewing, in which the interviewer is absorbed further into the 'life-world' of the interviewees such that the horizons of the research are framed as much by the 'subjects' as participants as by the researcher as expert, can be useful (Spradley, 1979). A potential problem with an ethnographic style here is that rather than taking on trust what interviewees say, discourse analysis attends to every word with a *suspicious* eye. In qualitative studies, the position of the researcher, and the way in which research knowledge is used, are foregrounded (Bell and Roberts, 1984). This does not mean, however, that issues of power are necessarily addressed. A radical study of discourse dynamics, on the other hand, would do this as a matter of course.

At some point with all recorded material decisions will have to be made about transcription conventions. The simplest are those given in the appendix of Potter and Wetherell (1987), though it is as well to be aware of alternative, more complex, varieties discussed in Brown and Yule (1983) and problems of levels of accuracy which arise when transcribing your own speech and that of someone else (Stubbs, 1983). The work on transcription conventions has been discussed most fully, not surprisingly, in the conversation analysis literature (Atkinson and Heritage, 1984). I have found the following transcription conventions sufficient:

1 when there are doubts about the accuracy of material, put it in round brackets (like this);
2 when material has been omitted from the transcript, signal it by putting a pair of empty square brackets, thus [ ];
3 when you need to clarify something, put the explanation in square brackets, like so [to help the reader];
4 when there are noises, words of assent, and so on, put this in slashes /hmm/, like this /yes/;

The following conventions are useful, though care should be taken that these, an artefact of transcription reflecting *interpretation* of the material on the part of the researcher, should not be seen as windows through which we may divine the true intentions of the speaker(s):

5 indicate the absence of a gap between one speaker and another
   with = marks at the end of one and the beginning of the next
   utterance;
6 indicate pauses in the speech with seconds in round brackets, e.g.,
   (2) for two seconds, and a full stop for small pauses less than a
   second, (.);
7 indicate an extended sound with colon marks, ye::s;
8 indicate emphases in speech by <u>underlining</u> those parts of the text;
9 indicate an intake of breath before a word by putting a full stop
   before it, .aah.

Although many versions of 'discourse analysis' outside psychology
have got caught in the trap of trying to formalise the analysis (turning
it eventually, in many cases, into a quantitative methodological
technique), the discussions of problems with transcription in that
literature are still useful (e.g., Stubbs, 1983).

It is possible to take visual texts and to elaborate the meanings in
spoken or written language such that the discourses that inhabit them
can be picked out. Here, the tradition of semiology is useful, and the
interpretations offered by Barthes (1973) of various icons of French
life can work as a guide. An accessible, and enjoyable, introduction
to the types of interpretation that you may employ at this stage will
be found in the essays by Williamson (1986). Images can be used to
provoke discussion, and so to elicit material (e.g., White and
Wetherell, 1988), but the actual discourse analysis of the images
themselves (advertisements, etc.) would involve the researcher in the
study of what Barthes (1973) called 'myth'. Stages two to five of
Potter and Wetherell's (1987) ten stages could be considered under
this heading.

'Analysis'

The identification of discourses can be aided by content analysis
(Mostyn, 1985) (and there is now an 'Ethnograph' word-processing
package which can select, collate and paste terms and phrases
quickly), but it is important to discuss the way the terms which would
be picked out by this method are *grouped*. What sense do the terms
make as part of a way of speaking, as part of a particular vocabulary?
Here, the technical exercise has to be complemented by some

attempt to 'validate' the operation of the categories. It is worth taking the texts, and the discourses that have been identified, to people outside the study to see what sense the analysis makes to others. A problem with this, and it can be addressed only by considering the positions of co-researchers and other peer-participants in relation to the dominant culture and dependent subcultures, is that discourse analysis could end up merely describing and confirming common sense (Potter *et al.*, 1990). We should remember that the variability of discourse rests on *conflicts* over meanings and uses of language. The dynamics of discourse inhere in the conflicts between stories and those other ways of speaking that resist, resist even though they may not speak in full voice. (In the description of groupings, systems of terms, you will have to be consistent in your choice of and uses of the term 'discourses' or 'interpretative repertoires'.) It would be possible to take up some of the issues discussed in stages six to nine of Potter and Wetherell's (1987) ten stages in this section. It will be useful here to look for 'implicit' themes suggested by the *absence* of certain terms (Billig *et al.*, 1988), and for this work a degree of intuition *must* be deployed (Hollway, 1989).

'Discussion'

Issues which can be addressed in a discussion section will vary according to the material, but the following points (which I have supplemented here with some references which explore related questions) emerged from discussions among students carrying out undergraduate research projects in the Manchester Discourse Group: difficulties of transcription including ambiguities and different coding schemes (Stubbs, 1983); the implicit rules of interviews, particularly those which are made salient by research 'disasters' (Brenner, 1978); the position of the interviewer, relating to the knowledge of the interviewer as it goes beyond, before or after, the interview (Oakley, 1981); confidentiality, including a reflection on how far it is possible to be explicit about sources of material; the issue of power, how this was displayed, mitigated or transformed (Bhavnani, 1990a, 1990b); motivation and interests of the researcher, including an attempt to tackle the question 'why do you want to know?' (Hollway, 1989); the value of the project, if it is a contribution to the growth of knowledge or the validation and publication of experience; subjective involvement, which includes how the research made you feel and what strategies of distancing were used (Stanley and Wise, 1983); what the effects were of doing the research, which includes deliberate attempts to engage in 'action research' (Kelly, 1986); reflection on audiences for the research, including the institutional pressures which allow some things to be said by some, and others to be silenced (Burman, 1990b); and generally things going wrong being accounted for, treated as occasions for discussion (Reason and Rowan, 1981).

These areas are not special to discourse analysis. On the contrary, they have been important in qualitative research for years, and it is now necessary to ensure that they find their way into the development of the discourse literature.

EMPIRICAL STUDIES

Perhaps the best way to get a feel for forms of discourse is to look at how analysts actually deal with texts. The following selection is categorised according to the four different strands of work which focus on repertoires, power and subjectivity, rhetoric and reflexivity. This is an entirely artificial categorisation device, but one which is just less confusing than other ways of grouping the research.

Repertoires

I use this heading to indicate the tradition of work inspired by *Discourse and Social Psychology* (Potter and Wetherell, 1987), a book which includes a number of examples of scientists', racist and riot discourse.

Scientists

The work on scientists is represented in Potter and Mulkay (1985) where many of the examples are of biochemists' interpretative strategies, and this paper is additionally useful because it addresses the issues of constraints and possibilities for re-interpretation of accounts in interviews. There is also a paper by McKinlay and Potter (1987a) on the way notions of models are used. The Sociology of Scientific Knowledge is connected to a Foucauldian framework in Hicks and Potter's (forthcoming) study of citation analysis in the disciplining of science.

Psychologists

Much of the work on 'scientists'' discourse actually focuses on psychologists' attempts to be scientific (to speak how they think scientists speak), and appears, for example, in Potter (1985) where he looks at notions of testability, falsification and so on in the informal talk around sessions at a BPS conference. There is a study of the way 'mechanist' and 'humanist' categories were employed in the discussion periods at an international conference of psychologists discussing theoretical issues in Potter (1988b). A recurrent theme in many of the papers on science 'repertoires' (discourses) by Potter and co-writers is the use of Kuhnian notions of paradigm shifts, and the way psychologists handle those ideas (a symptom of the way the new-paradigm debates continue to nag away at the positivists' image of themselves). Social psychologists came under scrutiny in Potter and Mulkay's (1982) study of the repertoires used in a semi-formal small group where European social psychologists discussed applied research.

Personal construct theory

Potter (1987) explores the way a group of personal construct psychologists use 'empiricist' and 'contingent' repertoires to justify their research (and, intriguingly, uses the work of the (post-) structuralist Barthes to help the analysis along). The personal construct group, and further transcript analysis, is also the setting for Potter's (1988a) discussion of notions of reflexivity. (The pity in all this work is that the psychologists had their anonymity guaranteed.)

Racism

Wetherell and Potter's (forthcoming) *Mapping the Language of Racism* will be a key text, but there have been a number of papers by them on this theme. The issue is discussed, as part of an introduction to discourse, by Wetherell and Potter (1986, 1988). Specifically, the material is racism in New Zealand. Potter and Wetherell (1988a) look at the way attitudes of the Whites to the Maori people are constructed in such a way as to avoid blame or accusations of racism. The issue is inflected in further papers: on explanations of educational disadvantage and positive discrimination (Potter and Wetherell, 1989); in accounts of violence during the 1981 Springbok rugby tour of New Zealand (Wetherell and Potter 1989); and, in a helpful political intervention, on talk about apartheid at a time when a boycott was being debated in the BPS (Potter and Wetherell, 1988b).

Riots

The issue of race appears again in an analysis of the categories of 'race' and 'government cuts' in explanations of the 1980 Bristol 'riot' (Litton and Potter, 1985). These events are also analysed in papers which address issues of social identity (Potter and Reicher, 1987; Reicher and Potter, 1985), and the issue of 'community leaders' in the events is the topic in Potter and Halliday's (1990) paper.

Gender

Wetherell (1986) introduces the notion of linguistic repertoires to help analyses of gender (and also draws on literary theory here). The links between discourses of gender and work are made by Wetherell *et al.* (1987), in which equal opportunities is a focus, and by Marshall and Wetherell (1989) which focuses on careers. Marshall (1991) analyses the social construction of 'motherhood' in childcare and parenting manuals. She has also looked at the professional regulation of maternity in a study of accounts by midwives and health visitors (Marshall, forthcoming). A paper by White and Wetherell (1988) deals with accounts young women give of body image and weight.

Other

Potter and Collie (1989) focus on the repertoires used to construct and justify or disparage notions of community care. Riach's (1989) project also discussed this topic through analysis of interviews with mental health workers. Moir's (1990) thesis research looked at the use of discourse in job selection and career guidance. Bola's (1989) project picked through the accounts given in the BPS *Bulletin* at the time of the Burt affair. There is also material on case conferences in Australia, which focuses on clinical psychologists (Soyland, 1988), which is being continued in Britain, and on educational psychology case conferences (Warren, 1988; Marks, 1990).

Power and subjectivity

The research under this heading follows in the wake of the tradition opened up by the journal *Ideology and Consciousness* (later *I & C*) in the late 1970s and *Changing the Subject* (Henriques *et al.*, 1984). It includes the work of those who have retained an overt concern with power and political practice and with (Foucauldian) post-structuralist ideas. It is concerned with discourse dynamics. This is not to say that it should be counterposed to the other strands, but the focus is more on the nature and function of discourses at (simultaneously) a cultural and subjective level.

Sexuality

One of the most compelling illustrations of the positioning of selves in discourse, and the way this is intermeshed with power, is in Valerie Walkerdine's (1981) study of the verbal abuse by small boys of a woman primary-school teacher. Walkerdine links the discourses at work with a wider discussion of philosophy of education and teacher-training ideologies. Walkerdine (1984) picks through images of gender in girls' comics, and this work is developed in a later book chapter (Walkerdine, 1987) to include a discussion of the dangers of the 'discourse determinism' that, she admits, could have been the message of some in her (Walkerdine, 1981) account of teacher–pupil discourse. There is also a selection of Walkerdine's work in a recent edited book (Walkerdine, 1991). The link between what is spoken in example texts and the operation of discourse in relation to gender relations is made also by Wendy Hollway's (1982) thesis, and her material from this, on heterosexual couples, is to be found in her chapter in Henriques *et al.* (1984) and in Hollway (1989). Hollway's description of heterosexual couples' discourses is taken up and used by Pringle (1989: 1991) in a discussion of the relationships between secretaries and their bosses. There is a discussion of the implications for an understanding of male violence in Hollway (1981). Corinne Squire's (1989) survey of feminism in psychology is located in this discourse tradition, and Gavey (1989) provides an overview of these issues. Outside psychology altogether, the structure of the British Conservatives' discourse on the 'promotion of homosexuality' in local government is analysed well by Smith (1990). Recently, amid some dreadful research (Parker, 1989c), there have been some useful analyses of the way AIDS has been discursively constituted as a topic (e.g., Seidel, 1990), and Haraway (1989) uses a feminist Foucauldian framework for a study of the image of the immune system in 'postmodern science'.

Racism

Issues of gender, culture and 'race' intersect in Amina Mama's (1987) thesis, supervised by Wendy Hollway, and this material will be found in published form in Mama (forthcoming). There is a chapter in the Henriques *et al.* (1984) volume on racism. Connections between discourses of gender and colonialism are explored by Mills (1990). There have also been the following two studies of anti-Semitism which are closely informed by an attention to discourse (produced in a publishing collective which included Erica Burman): Cohen's (1984) book discusses the slippages that routinely occur on the Left between anti-Zionism and anti-Semitism; Seidel's (1986b) book focuses on language and traces the influence of Right-wing historians in rewriting accounts of the Holocaust.

Institutions

The links between discourses and institutional power are made with reference to cognitive psychology and militarism by John Bowers (1990), and there are attempts to draw attention to the role of institutions as sites of power limiting interpretation in Parker (1989a). Hicks and Potter's (forthcoming) analysis of citation accounts in the disciplining of science connects Foucauldian work with the Sociology of Scientific Knowledge. An issue where these issues are salient, particularly in the light of Foucault's (1971) history of 'madness', is in the area of mental health. There is an interesting attempt to tie notions of discourse to clinical practice in Banton *et al.* (1985). Fairclough's (1990) recent introduction to discourse analysis, coming from linguistics but addressing issues of ideology and power, focuses on consumer and psychotherapy discourses. There is a (feminist) discourse analysis of (feminist) psychotherapy in Burman (in press).

Literary and other work

Post-structuralist notions of discourse have found their way into psychology after (and often *via*) literary theory, and there are now examples of critical writing which address texts as 'literary' products susceptible to (discourse-sensitive) literary analysis. Ashton (1990) discussed the plays of Harold Pinter in this way as a dissertation component of a psychology degree and Miall (1990) has discussed literary works as they pertain to clinical understandings of 'affect'. The developments in literary theory were first relayed into psychology in the new-paradigm literature, and Harré's (1979, 1983) foundation works for a new social and individual psychology include, in passing, many references to literary examples. Recently this has been taken further in an attention to discursive 'positioning' of selves (Davies and Harré, 1990). Deconstruction, in a way closely linked to literary theory, has been advertised as a tool to tease apart 'everyday explanation' in a study of radio soap opera (Parker, 1988a). Squire (1990a) uses the notion of discourse to demystify social psychology and, in a looser sense of deconstruction, social psychology is subjected to critique in various papers in Parker and Shotter (1990). Outside psychology, but a useful source on popular culture, is Redhead's (1990) survey, not confined to Manchester style, of postmodern 'post-political pop'.

Rhetoric

Some of the material covered under the last heading could just as easily fit here, but I use this section to group together studies which trace the ideological functions of language without necessarily invoking either a conversational analytic notion of discourse (as a set of formal devices) or a post-structuralist description of discourses. The Billig et al. (1988) book provides a number of empirical studies (of education, health, prejudice and gender). Other related work is to be found in Billig's (1988d, 1990d) studies of the British royal family, in Ros Gill's (1991) work on gender, ideology and popular radio, in Mike Michael's (1986) work on masculinity and ordinary explanation and in Condor's (1988) paper on race stereotypes. Identity is the focus of Ullah's (1990) study of the rhetoric of second-generation Irish. The discourse of punk identity is explored by Widdicombe and Wooffitt (1990). Other work which is quite close to this style of work, in the sense of displaying an attention to the role of language in processes of argumentation (though, in other senses, quite different), are Stringer's (1990) study of textbook introductions to psychology and Sinason's (1989) study of the linguistics of 'equal opportunities'.

The Washington Discourse Analysis Group's work on the rhetoric of President Bush (WAUDAG, 1990) and on discourses of AIDS (WAUDAG, 1989) also connect with issues of representation and resistance.

Reflexivity

The roots of this strand lie in studies of science and in ethno-methodology. Gilbert and Mulkay (1984) provide a good introduction to this sociology of scientific knowledge work (not least because the notion of discourse outlined there is one that Potter and Wetherell (1987) take up). This is further elaborated by Mulkay (1985). The collection edited by Woolgar (1988b) contains some examples in a variety of forms which attempt to display, in their very writing, their constructed nature. The ways in which non-scientists perceive science and technology policy is discussed by Michael (forthcoming). The ethnomethodological strand, concerned with problematising taken-for-granted assumptions, is best approached via an 'empirical' example, and a good one is to be found in Smith's paper (1984) on the labelling of a person ('K') as 'mentally ill'. Other work carried out at York in this reflexive climate includes Wooffitt's (1988) work on accounts of the paranormal and Ashmore's (1985, 1989) sociology of the sociology of science. The conversation analysis strand, like all quantitative approaches, does turn up some interesting material, and there are good examples in Atkinson's (1984) work on the rhetorical devices (three-part lists and contrasts) in political speeches, and in Grady and Potter's (1985) discussion of some of these devices in a British general election. Potter's contribution to the Howitt *et al.* (1989) introduction to social psychology, curiously, dwells on this tradition of work. This brings us full circle to the 'repertoires' tradition in full flow.

DISCOURSE-ORIENTATED CRITIQUES OF OTHER APPROACHES

Discourse analysis has had to emerge through posing itself as a credible alternative to other approaches in psychology, and so there are some useful discussions of conceptual problems within the discipline now in the discourse literature.

Cognitive psychology

Cognitivist explanations, mainly focusing on accounts of prejudice, are tackled most thoroughly by Billig (1985, 1989b) through a discussion of the rhetorical devices used in speech to justify positions too sophisticated to justify reduction to schemas or suchlike. Cognitivism is tackled, with reference to politicians' memory problems, in Edwards and Potter's (1991) discussion of Neisser's ecological accounts. The public construction of 'facts' about 'memory' is explored at length in Edwards and Potter (in press). Cognitive psychology also comes under attack by Bowers (1990) who notes the not adventitious connections between hierarchical models of the mind and those of military technology. Sherrard (1988) looks at Chomsky's famous review of Skinner, and raises relevant issues here. Alternatives to cognitivism which argue the case for a (broadly Foucauldian) discourse-sensitive version of (Gibsonian) ecological psychology have been suggested by Michael and Still (forthcoming) and (in a version of Chapter 5 of this book coupled with critical responses) Parker (forthcoming).

Attitudes

The shortcomings of the concept of 'attitude' as an explanatory device are explored by Billig (1988a), and Potter and Wetherell (1987) deal with the problems fully in *Discourse and Social Psychology* along with role, trait and humanist accounts of personality.

Social representations

Potter and Wetherell (1987) take on social representations theory. Social representations are tackled as well: by Litton and Potter (1985) which draws on 'riot' data to show the drawbacks of the framework; by Potter and Litton (1985) which pits the concept of social representations against the notion of interpretative repertoire; by McKinlay and Potter (1987b) who provide a critique of social representations from an implicitly discourse stance; and by McKinlay *et al.* (1990). The rhetoric position is compared with social representations by Billig (1988b, 1990c). Bhavnani (1990b) contrasts her work on 'discursive configurations' with social representations in ethnographic and interviewing studies of youth in Britain. The latent cognitivism in social representations theory is tackled by Parker (1987a) and, in more explicit deconstructive spirit, by Parker (1989a).

Attribution theory

The study of 'ordinary explanation' was dealt with by Michael (1986) in a series of studies which drew on the ideas that have since been explored by researchers concerned with power and subjectivity. Some of this thesis work appears in published form in Michael (1989). Parker (1989a) attempts an historically grounded deconstruction of attribution theory and the new-paradigm responses to it, and there is now a patient unravelling of the problems underlying attribution accounts by Potter and Edwards (1990) in which the critique revolves around ex-chancellor Lawson's memory failures after a journalists' lobby briefing on benefit cuts for old-aged pensioners.

Intergroup theory

The Tajfel legacy (Social Identity Theory) has not been subjected to a thorough discourse critique (Wetherell has thesis research and publications in that area), though there is the basis for one in a paper by Reicher and Potter (1985). (Reicher also has thesis research and a publication record in this tradition.) Griffin's (1989) critique of the approach is also informed by a discourse background, and Ullah's (1990) study of the rhetoric of second-generation Irish explores the limits of the social identity framework. Widdicombe and Wooffitt (1990) situate their analyses of punk identity in 'social comparison' debates, and tackle the intergroup theory framework head-on in analyses of punk and goth identity accounts in another paper (Wooffitt and Widdicombe, 1990). There is a section on the problems in the approach for an understanding of racism by Henriques in Henriques *et al.* (1984), and there is a good deconstructive assault on the approach by Michael (1990). *Deconstructing Social Psychology* (Parker and Shotter, 1990) contains a number of critical chapters on different aspects of social psychology in general.

OTHER INTRODUCTORY TEXTS AND SOURCES

'Introductions to discourse analysis' will be unhelpful as a general rule, though you will know as soon as you pick them up if they are giving an introduction to one of the varieties of discourse analysis in linguistics or socio-linguistics (e.g., Brown and Yule, 1983; Coulthard, 1977; Coulthard and Montgomery, 1981; Stubbs, 1983). The aim of most of these versions seems to be a desperate attempt to subject language to quantifiable formal(ist) analysis. There is also a tradition of work called discourse analysis which is unashamedly cognitive (e.g., Bromberg, 1990) and/or biologically based (e.g., Joanette and Brownell, 1990). A good account of the recent thinking of the ex-University of East Anglia team (Fowler, Hodge, Kress and Trew) will be found in Hodge and Kress (1988).

Papers

Apart from useful books by Potter and Wetherell (1987), Billig *et al.* (1988) and Hollway (1989) (together with Leith and Myerson's (1989) introduction to rhetoric from outside psychology and Fairclough's (1990) excellent introduction to Foucault's and Pêcheux's work from a linguistic direction), there are some helpful briefer introductions to this work. Two of the chapters in the Antaki (1988) volume – by Billig (1988c) on rhetoric and politically driven analysis (which is glossed, presumably tactically, under the rubric of 'scholarship') as opposed to the seemingly inevitable methods fetish in most research and by Wetherell and Potter (1988) on discourse analysis applied to New Zealand racists – are designed as introductions and empirical examples, and work well. There is an introductory overview of discourse analysis by Lalljee and Widdicombe (1989) in *Psychology Survey 7* which covers the Potter and Wetherell work and its roots in sociology of science (but which also connects it all rather too closely to conversation analysis). The ethogenic tradition is turning its attention to the organisation of language now, and there is a lucid extension of this approach to consider the positioning of the self in discourse by Davies and Harré (1990). The introduction to the Woolgar (1988b) edited collection *Knowledge and Reflexivity* is a good way in to reflexive issues.

Journals

Work has been trickling into the social psychology journals like *British Journal of Social Psychology* and, more slowly, *European Journal of Social Psychology*, but as empirical research with little prospect for theoretical debate. *Text* (edited by Tuen van Dijk who has recently moved closer to qualitative approaches) has included a number of discourse-analytic studies in recent years, though the 1990 special anniversary issue, 'looking ahead: discourse analysis in the 1990s', seems to see the future of the journal as tied to linguistics with a dab or two of conversation analysis. It is possible that *Journal for the Theory of Social Behaviour* (set up by Harré and Secord in 1972 in the heyday of the new-paradigm debates) will be a forum for a discussion of the turn to discourse. New journals *Theory and Psychology* (co-edited by Potter) and *Feminism and Psychology* (open to developments in qualitative theory and research) are likely to feature discourse material (e.g., Burman, 1990d). The key site for discourse data and debates, however, will be *Discourse & Society* which started in July 1990. (My cut-off date for the inclusion of references from this journal in this guide was the beginning of 1991.)

Contacts

Activities of Discourse Groups in Britain are described by Ashmore (1985, 1989), Potter (1989, 1990) and Parker (1991a). Different Discourse Groups can be traced at the following addresses: Discourse and Representations Group (an administrative convenience rather than a functioning group, but an important link between psychology and debates in cultural theory) c/o Margaret Wetherell, Department of Social Science, Open University, Milton Keynes MK7 6AN; Discourse Group (influenced by feminist, Foucauldian and Marxist theory, and connecting discourse research with politics in edited work (Burman and Parker, forthcoming) which will contain further examples of good research by Gill, Kirkwood, McNaghten, Marks, Marshall, Moir, Stenner and Widdicombe not referenced in this guide) c/o Erica Burman, Department of Psychology and Speech Pathology, Manchester Polytechnic, Hathersage Road, Manchester M13 0JA; Discourse and Rhetoric Group (which compiles an up-to-date reference list of publications by its members, and so is worth contacting for a full picture of the Billig, Potter, Wetherell *et al.* work) c/o Michael Billig, Department of Social Sciences, Loughborough University of Technology, Loughborough, Leicestershire LE11 3TU; Discourse Analysis Research Group (which produces the useful *DARG Newsletter*, based on Canadian/North American activities but also reporting on work in Europe) c/o

Newsletter Editor, Education Tower 1428, 2500 University Drive, N.W., Calgary AB, Canada, T2N 1N4; Hermeneutics, Rhetoric and Discourse Analysis Research Group c/o Professor Lorant Bencze, Lorand Eotvos University, Budapest H-1364, Pesti, B.u.l. Pf. 107, Hungary.

CRITICAL RESPONSES

Psychology has dealt with discourse analysis so far by ignoring it and hoping it will go away. There are few critiques from within the dominant experimental tradition. It is entirely possible that positivist psychologists think that they said all that was to be said to the new-paradigm psychologists in the 1970s. Since most of the responses then (wrongly) targeted the supposed return to introspection, this is all the more disappointing. The new main introductory social psychology textbook (Hewstone et al., 1988) published in Britain does not, and nor did its predecessor (Tajfel and Fraser, 1978), mention Harré, Shotter or the new-paradigm debates, let alone discourse analysis. The numerous American psychology texts, of course, do not mention these ideas. The judgement of the still dominant 'old paradigm' was well expressed recently as follows: 'There was little "research" of a recognisable kind, but a lot of talk and writing.... These ideas have had little practical application' (Argyle, 1989: 16). A good general critique of the *dangers* of qualitative research and simple 'empowerment' of the researched which appeared then, however, is by the now discourse-rhetorical Billig (1977). Billig's (1987) turn to rhetoric is sympathetically but rigorously reviewed by Reicher (1988) who locates the general many-sided argumentative nature of thought Billig proposes in a historical context. Billig *et al.*'s (1988) *Ideological Dilemmas* is reviewed by Spears (1989).

Discourse and Social Psychology (Potter and Wetherell, 1987) is discussed in a long essay review by Bowers (1988) from a post-structuralist position. As well as focusing on the failure to include dialogical examples with the researcher's own interventions, Bowers raises the problem of the 'unitary subject' in their account. The problem of validating discourse analysis is discussed with an eye to Bourdieu's work by Sherrard (1991). There is a scathing review of conceptual and political problems with the practice of discourse analysis by Burman (in press b). The Foucauldian twist to discourse connecting it with power and resistance appears in the journal *Philosophical Psychology* (Parker, 1990a), and this is criticised by Potter *et al.* (1990) and attacked by Abrams and Hogg (1990) arguing from a fairly traditional positivist position. There is a review of Parker's (1989a) attempt to use Derridian and Foucauldian theory to find a way out of the crisis in modern social psychology by Hopkins (1990). A good (as could be hoped for, given the way the traditional categories are relentlessly subverted) review of Ashmore's (1989) reflexive thesis is by the sociologist of science Collins (1990).

THEORETICAL ISSUES

Discourse has been explored for some time outside psychology, and the most interesting theoretical problems have been debated there. What follows here is a selection of texts which deal with some of these issues grouped under the headings of continental philosophy, realism and psychoanalysis.

Continental philosophy

The tradition of philosophical writing in France and Germany this century has taken a very different tack to that of Anglo-American work. Against 'common-sense' analytic philosophy and pragmatism, continental theory has included complex, sometimes arcane discussions of the meaning of meaning. The tension between existentialist and structuralist traditions on the continent has transformed itself many times, and is expressed now in, among other forms, the opposition between critical theory and postmodernism. The best overall appraisal of the debates in both these traditions is by Dews (1987), though this is not a good place to start.

The Posties

Post-structuralist ideas are notoriously difficult to summarise, and often accounts involve a long detour through the problems of phenomenology and the rise of structuralism before the ideas of the main writers (Derrida, Foucault, Lacan) are arrived at. A lucid introduction, a good place to start, is provided by Sarup (1988). The philosophical underpinnings of the work are explored, for those with a background in the discipline, in Descombes (1980). There is a good account of post-structuralist views of discourse in Macdonell (1986) which traces a route through Althusser and Hindess and Hirst to arrive at Foucault, and an excellent defence of the relevance of post-structuralist theory for feminism in Weedon (1987). A lucid introduction to the place of post-structuralism in literary theory is provided by Eagleton (1983), and a good political defence of these ideas will be found in Belsey (1980). Easthope (1988) provides an overview of the development of post-structuralism in Britain since 1968, and a clear account of some the key ideas along the way. The disciplines covered include English literature, art history, cultural studies, the social sciences and psychology (in which he takes *Changing the Subject* to task). *The Crisis in Modern Social Psychology* (Parker 1989a) and *Deconstructing Social Psychology* (Parker and Shotter, 1990) explain and use post-structuralist ideas.

Changing the Subject (Henriques *et al.*, 1984) is the first thorough (complex) application of post-structuralism to psychology, and should be read, though perhaps after two other books by co-authors: Walkerdine (1988) uses the ideas to discuss the development of 'reason' in the child, and Hollway (1989) develops the ideas clearly in relation to a (broadly Foucauldian) version of discourse analysis. Gavey (1989) provides an overview of the relationship between feminism, post-structuralism and discourse analysis.

The interest in the constitutive power of language in post-structuralist work mutated recently into a series of claims about the state of culture in which this work could seem plausible and attractive. Postmodernism is now sometimes used as a code-word for post-structuralism, and the type of culture in which all meaning shifts and slips as fast as post-structuralists think it does is postmodernity. The classic text for discussions of postmodernity is Lyotard's (1984), but a better introduction is to be found in the Jameson (1984) article. The Doherty *et al.* (1991) collection provides an overview of the development of postmodernism in the social sciences, with contributions on sociology, geography and international relations. In this volume there are papers by Bowers (1991) on cognitive psychology, Burman (1991) on developmental psychology and Parker (1991b) on social psychology.

The most useful attacks on post-structuralism, alongside spirited defences of modernity, are by Habermas (1981) and followers. The Billig *et al.* (1988) volume mentions Habermas only in passing (and not favourably), but is the closest in discourse theory in psychology at the moment to a Habermasian position. The best philosophical assessment of the posties from the critical theory tradition is still Dews (1987).

Journals

These ideas, as with new qualitative approaches in psychology, have been fired by feminism, and an excellent new American journal, *differences*, has already, since starting in 1989, included Foucauldian styles of discourse analysis. (It does look as if it might get a bit heavy on the theory from time to time, a risk all texts in this area take.) Three new relevant journals were launched by Routledge in 1987: *New Formations* views culture through a post-structuralist lens, and has already contained some interesting discourse work; *Cultural Studies* focuses on popular culture, and is explicitly concerned with theories of discourse and power; *Textual Practice* is pitched at a literary theory audience, but is worth browsing through to get a sense of the direction of debates (which may one day seep into psychology). These journals are sensitive to issues of racism as well as gender, but there is also a need for journals such as *Third Text* which take up race, colonialism and anti-racist politics as they are mediated by discourse.

Realism

The relativism which post-structuralism seems to entail is discussed from a Marxist standpoint, alongside a consideration of Habermas, by Anderson (1983), and radicals worried about the dangers of relativism have turned to debates in the philosophy of science (and now social science) over the value of realism.

A clear exposition of the critical realist position will be found in the first chapter of Bhaskar (1989), though the other chapters can be heavy-going. There is also a good overview by Outhwaite (1987) which compares the realist position with that of hermeneutics and critical theory. There is a clear review of the realist as opposed to three other views of social structure by Porpora (1989), and another good account by Isaac (1990) which is marred, though, by a bizarre attempt to argue that realism is, in some way, postmodern. Both of these papers appear in *Journal for the Theory of Social Behaviour* which was set up as a forum for debate by Harré and Secord, and which has often carried useful papers on realist debates in social science.

The various political implications of the discourse position once it becomes disconnected from a form of materialism can be traced on the Left in Laclau and Mouffe's (1985) avowedly 'post-Marxist' text, and in Seidel's (1986a) account of the Right's use of Gramsci and discourse theory deliberately to recast the terms of debate over culture and 'race'. There is a thorough, caustic response to the Laclau and Mouffe argument by Geras (1987), and an (even angrier) exchange follows from this (Laclau and Mouffe, 1987; Geras, 1988). The worst political implications of post-structuralism have been explored well: Dews (1979) shows how Foucault was taken up by some of the (Maoist) far Left in France and mutated into a version of the far Right; Stern (1990) works through some of the consequences of Derrida's response to the discovery that De Man, a (dead) prominent American deconstructionist published in pro-Vichy papers during the war.

Psychoanalysis

Wendy Hollway (1989) uses Lacanian approaches in a clear way (unusually for this material), and also brings in a Kleinian account of defence mechanisms in her interpretation of the discourse of heterosexual couples talking about their relationships. She quotes Stephen Frosh (1987) a lot, and his book is a clear outline of Freudian and post-Freudian theory (including some object-relations, Reichian and post-Lacanian writing). Frosh (1989b) also has some useful material on psychoanalysis and discourse in a chapter on gender and language. There is a full length essay review of Hollway's book by Widdicombe (1990) which is both critical and sympathetic. The production of the 'ego' in psychoanalytic discourse is discussed by Parker (in press).

Another example, which traces the symbolic and emotional resonances of equal opportunities language using psychoanalysis, is to be found in Sinason (1989). Psychoanalysis is connected in a more difficult theoretical way by Henriques et al. (1984), and this includes fascinating work by Urwin connecting Lacanian and Foucauldian accounts of language. The connections between post-Kleinian psychoanalysis and postmodernism are explored by Rustin (1989), and the possible realist basis for psychoanalysis in practice is discussed by Rustin (1987). Reflexivity and psychoanalysis are also discussed in relation to a piece of empirical research in Walkerdine

(1986). The most useful journal, one which is heavily slanted to the Kleinian and object-relations tradition but which contains articles by writers sympathetic to Habermas and those working through Lacan's work, is *Free Associations*.

References

Abrams, D. and Hogg, M.A. (1990) 'The context of discourse: let's not throw out the baby with the bathwater', *Philosophical Psychology* 3 (2): 219–25.

Adorno, T. and Horkheimer, M. (1944/1979) *Dialectic of Enlightenment*, London: Verso.

Althusser, L. (1971) *Lenin and Philosophy and Other Essays*, London: New Left Books.

Andersen, R. (1988) *The Power and the Word: Language, Power and Change*, London: Paladin.

Anderson, P. (1983) *In the Tracks of Historical Materialism*, London: Verso.

Anderson, P. (1984) 'Modernity and revolution', *New Left Review* 144: 96–113.

Antaki, C. (ed.) (1988) *Analysing Everyday Explanation: A Casebook of Methods*, London: Sage.

Argyle, M. (1989) 'British social psychology (as I saw it)', *BPS Social Psychology Section Newsletter* 21: 15–19.

Ashmore, M. (1985) 'A question of reflexivity: Wrighting sociology of scientific knowledge', unpublished D.Phil. thesis, University of York.

Ashmore, M. (1989) *The Reflexive Thesis: Wrighting Sociology of Scientific Knowledge*, Chicago: University of Chicago Press.

Ashton, M. (1990) 'An account of a psychological approach to Harold Pinter (with hardly a mention of Freud)', unpublished B.Sc. dissertation, Manchester Polytechnic.

Atkinson, J.M. (1984) *Our Masters' Voices: The Language and Body Language of Politics*, London: Methuen.

Atkinson, J.M. and Heritage, J.C. (eds) (1984) *Structures of Social Action: Studies in Conversation Analysis*, Cambridge: Cambridge University Press.

Austin, J.L. (1962) *How to Do Things with Words*, Oxford: Clarendon Press.

Back, K.W. (1989) 'Thriller: the self in modern society', in J. Shotter and K.J. Gergen (eds) *Texts of Identity*, London and New York: Sage.

Banton, R., Clifford, P., Frosh, S., Lousada, J. and Rosenthall, J. (1985) *The Politics of Mental Health*, London: Macmillan.

Barrett, M. and McIntosh, M. (1982) *The Anti-Social Family*, London: Verso.

Barthes, R. (1973) *Mythologies*, London: Paladin.

Barthes, R. (1977) *Image–Music–Text*, London: Fontana.

Barthes, R. (1990) *A Lover's Discourse*, London: Fontana.
Bates, B. (1983) *The Way of Wyrd*, London: Century Publishing.
Bauman, Z. (1988a) 'Sociology and postmodernity', *Sociological Review* 36 (4): 790–813.
Bauman, Z. (1988b) 'Is there a postmodern sociology?', *Theory, Culture and Society* 5 (2/3): 217–37.
Bell, C. and Roberts, H. (eds) (1984) *Social Researching: Politics, Problems, Practice*, London: Routledge & Kegan Paul.
Bell, D. (1965) *The End of Ideology: On the Exhaustion of Political Ideas in the Fifties*, New York: Free Press.
Belsey, C. (1980) *Critical Practice*, London: Methuen.
Berger, P.L. and Luckmann, T. (1971) *The Social Construction of Reality: A Treatise in the Sociology of Knowledge*, Harmondsworth: Penguin.
Berman, M. (1983) *All That Is Solid Melts Into Air: The Experience of Modernity*, London: Verso.
Bettelheim, B. (1986) *Freud and Man's Soul*, London: Flamingo.
Bhaskar, R. (1978) A Realist Theory of Science (2nd Edn), Brighton: Harvester.
Bhaskar, R. (1989) *Reclaiming Reality: A Critical Introduction to Contemporary Philosophy*, London: Verso.
Bhavnani, K-K. (1990a) 'What's power got to do with it? Empowerment and social research', in I. Parker and J. Shotter (eds) *Deconstructing Social Psychology*, London: Routledge.
Bhavnani, K-K. (1990b) *Talking Politics: A Psychological Framing for Views from Youth in Britain*, Cambridge: Cambridge University Press.
Billig, M. (1977) 'The new social psychology and "fascism"', *European Journal of Social Psychology* 7: 393–432.
Billig, M. (1982) *Ideology and Social Psychology: Extremism, Moderation and Contradiction*, Oxford: Blackwell.
Billig, M. (1985) 'Prejudice, categorization and particularization: from a perceptual to a rhetorical approach', *European Journal of Social Psychology* 15: 79–103.
Billig, M. (1987) *Arguing and Thinking: A Rhetorical Approach to Social Psychology*, Cambridge: Cambridge University Press.
Billig, M. (1988a) 'Rhetorical and historical aspects of attitudes: the case of the British monarchy', *Philosophical Psychology* 1: 83–104.
Billig, M. (1988b) 'Social representation, objectification and anchoring: a rhetorical analysis', *Social Behaviour* 3: 1–16.
Billig, M. (1988c) 'Methodology and scholarship in understanding ideological explanation', in C. Antaki (ed.) *Analysing Everyday Explanation: A Casebook of Methods*, London: Sage.
Billig, M. (1988d) 'Common-places of the British royal family: a rhetorical analysis of plain and argumentative sense', *Text* 8: 91–110.
Billig, M. (1989a) 'The argumentative nature of holding strong views: a case study', *European Journal of Social Psychology* 19: 203–23.
Billig, M. (1989b) 'Psychology, rhetoric, and cognition', *History of the Human Sciences* 2: 289–307.
Billig, M. (1990a) 'Rhetoric of social psychology', in I. Parker and J. Shotter (eds) *Deconstructing Social Psychology*, London: Routledge.

Billig, M. (1990b) 'Collective memory, ideology and the British royal family', in D. Middleton and D. Edwards (eds) *Collective Remembering*, London: Sage.

Billig, M. (1990c) 'Studying the thinking society: social representations, rhetoric and attitudes', in G. Breakwell and D. Canter (eds) *Empirical Approaches to Social Representations*, Oxford: Oxford University Press.

Billig, M. (1990d) 'Stacking the cards of ideology: the history of the *Sun Souvenir Royal Album*', *Discourse & Society* 1 (1): 17–37.

Billig, M., Condor, S., Edwards, D., Gane, M., Middleton, D. and Radley, A. (1988) *Ideological Dilemmas: A Social Psychology of Everyday Thinking*, London: Sage.

Bola, M. (1989) 'A study of discourse in accounts given over the Cyril Burt "Affair" ', unpublished B.Sc. project, Manchester Polytechnic.

Bowers, J. (1988) 'Essay review of *Discourse and Social Psychology*', *British Journal of Social Psychology* 27: 185–92.

Bowers, J. (1990) 'All hail the great abstraction: Star Wars and the politics of cognitive psychology', in I. Parker and J. Shotter (eds) *Deconstructing Social Psychology*, London and New York: Routledge.

Bowers, J. (1991) 'Postmodernity and the globalisation of technoscience: the computer, cognitive science and war', in J. Doherty, E. Graham and M. Malek (eds) *Postmodernism and the Social Sciences*, London: Macmillan.

Brenner, M. (1978) 'Interviewing: the social phenomenology of a research instrument', in M. Brenner, P. Marsh and M. Brenner (eds) *The Social Contexts of Method*, London: Croom Helm.

Bromberg, M. (1990) 'Advance planning of discourse in potential exchange situations', *European Journal of Social Psychology* 20: 77–84.

Brown, G. and Yule, G. (1983) *Discourse Analysis*, Cambridge: Cambridge University Press.

Burman, E. (1989) 'Feminists and feminisms in psychology', paper given at British Psychological Society conference, London, December.

Burman, E. (1990a) 'Differing with deconstruction: a feminist critique', in I. Parker and J. Shotter (eds) *Deconstructing Social Psychology*, London: Routledge.

Burman, E. (1990b) (ed.) *Feminists and Psychological Practice*, London: Sage.

Burman, E. (1990c) 'Power, gender and developmental psychology', *Feminism and Psychology* 1 (1):

Burman, E. (1991) 'Developmental psychology and the postmodern child', in J. Doherty, E. Graham and M. Malek (eds) *Postmodernism and the Social Sciences*, London: Macmillan.

Burman, E. (in press a) 'Discourses of feminist psychotherapy: Authenticity, identification and power', in J. Siegfried (ed.) *Therapeutic and Everyday Discourse as Behavior Change: Towards a micro-analysis in psychotherapy process research*, New York: Ablex.

Burman, E. (in press b) 'What discourse is not', *Philosophical Psychology*.

Burman, E. and Parker, I. (eds) (forthcoming) *Discourse Analytic Research: Repertoires and readings of texts in action*, London and New York: Routledge.

Carlen, P. (1986) 'Psychiatry in prisons: promises, premises, practices and politics', in P. Miller and N. Rose (eds) *The Power of Psychiatry*, Cambridge: Polity Press.

Cohen, S. (1984) *That's Funny, You Don't Look Anti-Semitic: An Anti-Racist Analysis of Left Anti-Semitism*, Leeds: Beyond the Pale Collective.

Cole, M. (1990) 'Preface', in D. Middleton and D. Edwards (eds) *Collective Remembering*, London and New York: Sage.

Collins, H. (1990) 'Tu quoque: review of Ashmore (1989)', *Times Higher Education Supplement*, 2 March: 20.

Collins, R. (1981) 'On the microfoundations of macrosociology', *American Journal of Sociology* 86: 984–1014.

Condor, S. (1988) '"Race stereotypes" and racist discourse', *Text* 8: 69–90.

Costall, A. (1984) 'Are theories of perception necessary? a review of Gibson's *The Ecological Approach to Visual Perception*', *Journal of the Experimental Analysis of Behavior* 1: 97–103.

Costall, A. and Still, A. (eds) (1987) *Cognitive Psychology in Question*, Hassocks, Sussex: Harvester.

Costall, A. and Still, A. (1989) 'Gibson's theory of direct perception and the problem of cultural relativism', *Journal for the Theory of Social Behaviour* 19 (4): 433–41.

Coulthard, M. (1977) *An Introduction to Discourse Analysis*, London: Longman.

Coulthard, M. and Montgomery, M. (eds) (1981) *Studies in Discourse Analysis*, London: Routledge & Kegan Paul.

Crellin, C. (1989) 'Plant psychology', unpublished ms., University of Liverpool.

Davies, B. and Harré, R. (1990) 'Positioning: the discursive production of selves', *Journal for the Theory of Social Behaviour* 20 (1): 43–63.

Deaux, K. and Wrightsman, L.S. (1984) *Social Psychology in 80s*, (4th Edn), Monterey, California: Brooks/Cole Publishing Company.

Deleuze, G. and Guattari, F. (1977) *Anti-Oedipus: Capitalism and Schizophrenia*, London: Viking.

Derrida, J. (1976) *Of Grammatology*, Baltimore: Johns Hopkins University Press.

Derrida, J. (1982) 'Sending: on representation', *Social Research* 49: 294–326.

Derrida, J. (1983) *Speech and Phenomena, and Other Essays on Husserl's Theory of Signs*, Evanston: Northwestern University Press.

Descombes, V. (1980) *Modern French Philosophy*, Cambridge: Cambridge University Press.

Dews, P. (1979) 'The *Nouvelle Philosophe* and Foucault', *Economy and Society* 8: 127–71.

Dews, P. (1987) *Logics of Disintegration: Post-structuralist Thought and the Claims of Critical Theory*, London: Verso.

Doherty, J., Graham, E. and Malek, M. (eds) (1991) *Postmodernism and the Social Sciences*, London: Macmillan.

Dreyfus, H.L. (1967) 'Why computers must have bodies in order to be intelligent', *Review of Metaphysics* 21: 13–32.

Eagleton, T. (1981) *Walter Benjamin, or, Towards a Revolutionary Criticism*, London: Verso.

Eagleton, T. (1983) *Literary Theory: An Introduction*, Oxford: Basil Blackwell.

Eagleton, T. (1985) 'Capitalism, modernism and postmodernism', *New Left Review* 152: 60–73.

Easthope, A. (1988) *British Post-structuralism, since 1968*, London: Routledge.

Easthope, A. (1990) '"I gotta use words when I talk to you": deconstructing the theory of communication', in I. Parker and J. Shotter (eds) *Deconstructing Social Psychology*, London: Routledge.

Edwards, D. and Potter, J. (1991) 'The Chancellor's Memory: Rhetoric and Truth in Discursive Remembering', *Applied Cognitive Psychology* 5:

Edwards, D. and Potter, J. (in press) *Discursive Psychology: From memory and attribution to fact construction and accountability*, London: Sage.

Evans, E.P. (1906/1987) *The Criminal Prosecution and Capital Punishment of Animals: The Lost History of Europe's Animal Trials*, London: Faber.

Fairclough, N. (1990) *Discourse Analysis*, Cambridge: Polity Press.

Farr, R.M. (1978) 'On the varieties of social psychology: an essay on the relationships between psychology and other social sciences', *Social Science Information* 17: 503–25.

Farr, R.M. and Moscovici, S. (eds) (1984) *Social Representations*, Cambridge: Cambridge University Press.

Fiske, S.T. and Taylor, S.E. (1984) *Social Cognition: Perspectives on Everyday Understanding*, Reading, Mass.: Addison-Wesley.

Foucault, M. (1970) *The Order of Things*, London: Tavistock.

Foucault, M. (1971) *Madness and Civilization: A History of Insanity in the Age of Reason*, London: Tavistock.

Foucault, M. (1972) *The Archaeology of Knowledge*, London: Tavistock.

Foucault, M. (1975) *I, Pierre Riviére, Having Slaughtered my Mother, my Sister, and my Brother . . .*, New York: Random House.

Foucault, M. (1977) *Discipline and Punish*, London: Allen Lane.

Foucault, M. (1980) *Power/Knowledge: Selected Interviews and Other Writings 1972–1977*, Hassocks, Sussex: Harvester.

Foucault, M. (1981) *The History of Sexuality Vol I: An Introduction*, Harmondsworth: Penguin.

Frazer, E. (1988) 'Teenage girls talking about class', *Sociology* 22 (3): 343–58.

Freud, S. (1905) *Three Essays on the Theory of Sexuality*, SE VII.

Freud, S. (1925) 'A note upon the "mystic writing pad" ', SE XIX.

Freud, S. (1953–74) *The Standard Edition of the Complete Psychological Works of Sigmund Freud* (24 vols), ed. J. Strachey, London: Hogarth Press and the Institute of Psycho-Analysis.

Frosh, S. (1987) *The Politics of Psychoanalysis: An Introduction to Freudian and Post-Freudian Theory*, London: Macmillan.

Frosh, S. (1989a) 'Melting into air: psychoanalysis and social experience', *Free Associations* 16: 7–30.

Frosh, S. (1989b) *Psychoanalysis and Psychology: Minding the Gap*, London: Macmillan.

Garfinkel, H. (1967) *Studies in Ethnomethodology*, New York: Prentice-Hall.

Gauld, A.O. and Shotter, J. (1977) *Human Action and its Psychological Investigation*, London: Routledge & Kegan Paul.

Gavey, N. (1989) 'Feminist poststructuralism and discourse analysis: contributions to a feminist psychology', *Psychology of Women Quarterly* 4: 459–75.

Geras, N. (1987) 'Post-Marxism?', *New Left Review* 163: 40–82.

Geras, N. (1988) 'Ex-Marxism without substance: being a real reply to Laclau and Mouffe', *New Left Review* 169: 34–61.

Gergen, K.J. (1973) 'Social psychology as history', *Journal of Personality and Social Psychology* 26: 309–20.

Gergen, K.J. (1982) *Toward Transformation in Social Knowledge*, New York: Springer Verlag.

Gergen, K.J. (1985) 'The social constructionist movement in modern psychology', *American Psychologist* 40: 266–75.

Gibson, J.J. (1966) *The Senses Considered as Perceptual Systems*, Boston: Houghton Mifflin.

Gibson, J.J. (1967) 'James J. Gibson', in E.G. Boring and G. Lindzey (eds) *A History of Psychology in Autobiography V*, New York: Appleton-Century-Crofts.

Gibson, J.J. (1979) *The Ecological Approach to Visual Perception*, Boston: Houghton Mifflin.

Giddens, A. (1979) *Central Problems in Social Theory: Action, Structure and Contradiction in Social Analysis*, London: Macmillan.

Gilbert, N. and Mulkay, M. (1984) *Opening Pandora's Box: A Sociological Analysis of Scientists' Discourse*, Cambridge: Cambridge University Press.

Gill, R. (1991) 'Ideology and popular radio: a discourse analytic examination of disc jockeys' talk', unpublished Ph.D. thesis, Loughborough University of Technology.

Goffman, E. (1968) *Asylums*, Harmondsworth: Penguin.

Goffman, E. (1971) *The Presentation of Self in Everyday Life*, Harmondsworth: Penguin.

Gordon, I.E. (1989) *Theories of Visual Perception*, Chichester: Wiley.

Grady, K. and Potter, J. (1985) 'Speaking and clapping: a comparison of Foot and Thatcher's oratory', *Language and Communication* 5: 173–83.

Green, D. (1989) 'Tales of discovery: narrative approaches to training clinical psychologists', *BPS Psychotherapy Section Newsletter* 7: 28–36.

Griffin, C. (1989) ' I'm not a women's libber but . . . : feminism, consciousness and identity', in S. Skevington and D. Baker (eds) *The Social Identity of Women*, London: Sage.

Grünbaum, A. (1984) *The Foundations of Psychoanalysis: A Philosophical Investigation*, Berkeley: University of California Press.

Habermas, J. (1970) 'On systematically distorted communication', *Inquiry* 13: 205–18.

Habermas, J. (1971) *Knowledge and Human Interests*, London: Heinemann.

Habermas, J. (1981) 'Modernity vs. post-modernism', *New German Critique* 22: 375–87.

Habermas, J. (1985) 'A philosophico-political profile', *New Left Review* 151: 75–105.

Haraway, D. (1989) 'The biopolitics of postmodern bodies: determinations of self in immune systems discourse', *Differences* 1 (1): 3–43. Reprinted in D. Haraway, *Simians, Cybergs and Women: The Reinvention of Nature*, London: Free Association Books.

Hare-Mustin, R.T. and Maracek, J. (1988) 'The meaning of difference: gender theory, postmodernism, and psychology', *American Psychologist* 43 (6): 455–64.

Harré, R. (1970) *Philosophies of Science: An Introductory Survey*, Oxford: Oxford University Press.

Harré, R. (1979) *Social Being: A Theory for Social Psychology*, Oxford: Basil Blackwell.

Harré, R. (1983) *Personal Being: A Theory for Individual Psychology*, Oxford: Basil Blackwell.

Harré, R. (1985) 'Review of J. Potter, P. Stringer and M. Wetherell (1984)', *Psychology News* 42: 20.

Harré, R. (ed.) (1986a) *The Social Construction of Emotions*, Oxford: Basil Blackwell.

Harré, R. (1986b) *Varieties of Realism*, Oxford: Basil Blackwell.

Harré, R., Clarke, D. and De Carlo, N. (1985) *Motives and Mechanisms: An Introduction to the Psychology of Action*, London: Methuen.

Harré, R. and Secord, P.F. (1972) *The Explanation of Social Behaviour*, Oxford: Basil Blackwell.

Hassan, I. (1985) 'The culture of postmodernism', *Theory, Culture and Society* 2 (3): 119–31.

Hebdige, D. (1979) *Subculture: The Meaning of Style*, London: Methuen.

Henriques, J., Hollway, W., Urwin, C., Venn, C. and Walkerdine, V. (1984) *Changing the Subject: Psychology, Social Regulation and Subjectivity*, London: Methuen.

Heseltine, M. (1990) quoted in the *Guardian*, April 21.

Hewstone, M., Stroebe, W., Codol, J.-P. and Stephenson, G.M. (eds) (1988) *Introduction to Social Psychology*, Oxford: Basil Blackwell.

Hicks, D. and Potter, J. (forthcoming) 'Sociology of scientific knowledge – A reflexive citation analysis or: Science disciplines and disciplining science', *Social Studies of Science*.

Hodge, R. and Kress, G. (1988) *Social Semiotics*, Cambridge: Polity Press.

Hollway, W. (1981) ' "I just wanted to kill a woman." Why? The Ripper and male sexuality', *Feminist Review* 9: 33–44. Reprinted in Feminist Review (ed.) (1987) *Sexuality: A Reader*, London: Virago.

Hollway, W. (1982) 'Identity and gender difference in adult social relationships', unpublished Ph.D. thesis, University of London.

Hollway, W. (1989) *Subjectivity and Method in Psychology: Gender, Meaning and Science*, London: Sage.

Hopkins, N. (1990) 'Review of Parker (1989a)', *British Journal of Social Psychology* 29: 283–5.

Howitt, D., Billig, M., Cramer, D., Edwards, D., Kniveton, B., Potter, J. and Radley, A. (1989) *Social Psychology: Conflicts and Continuities*, Milton Keynes: Open University Press.

Isaac, J. (1990) 'Realism and reality: some realistic reconsiderations', *Journal for the Theory of Social Behaviour* 20 (1): 1–31.

Jameson, F. (1984) 'Postmodernism, or the cultural logic of late capitalism', *New Left Review* 146: 53–92.

Jay, M. (1973) *The Dialectical Imagination: A History of the Frankfurt School and the Institute of Social Research 1923–50*, London: Heinemann.

Joanette, Y. and Brownell, H.M. (eds) (1990) *Discourse Ability and Brain Damage: Theoretical and Empirical Perspectives*, London: Springer-Verlag.

Katz, S. (1987) 'Is Gibson a relativist?', in A. Costall and A. Still (eds) *Cognitive Psychology in Question*, Hassocks, Sussex: Harvester.

Kelly, A. (1986) 'Action research: what is it and what can it do?', in R. Burgess (ed.) *Issues in Educational Research: Qualitative Methods*, Hassocks, Sussex: Falmer Press.

Kline, P. (1984) *Psychology and Freudian Theory: An Introduction*, London: Methuen.

Lacan, J. (1977) *Écrits: A Selection*, London: Tavistock.

Lacan, J. (1979) *The Four Fundamental Concepts of Psycho-Analysis*, Harmondsworth: Penguin.

Laclau, E. and Mouffe, C. (1985) *Hegemony and Socialist Strategy: Towards a Radical Democratic Politics*, London: Verso.

Laclau, E. and Mouffe, C. (1987) 'Post-Marxism without apologies', *New Left Review* 166: 79–106.

Lalljee, M. and Widdicombe, S. (1989) 'Discourse analysis', in A.M. Colman and J.G. Beaumont (eds) *Psychology Survey 7*, London and Leicester: BPS and Routledge.

Lash, S. (1988) 'Discourse or figure? Postmodernism as "regime of signification" ', *Theory, Culture and Society* 5 (2/3): 311–36.

Lawson, H. (1984) *Reflexivity: The Postmodern Predicament*, London: Hutchinson.

Leith, D. and Myerson, G. (1989) *The Power of Address: Explorations in Rhetoric*, London: Routledge.

Litton, I. and Potter, J. (1985) 'Social representations in the ordinary explanation of a "riot" ', *European Journal of Social Psychology* 15: 371–88.

Löwy, M. (1988) 'Marxism and liberation theology', *Notebooks for Study and Research/ Cahiers d'Etude et de Recherche* 10.

Lyotard, J.-F. (1984) *The Postmodern Condition: A Report on Knowledge*, Manchester: Manchester University Press.

Macdonell, D. (1986) *Theories of Discourse: An Introduction*, Oxford: Basil Blackwell.

MacIntyre, A. (1981) *After Virtue*, London: Duckworth.

McKinlay, A. and Potter, J. (1987a) 'Model discourse: interpretative repertoires in scientists' conference talk', *Social Studies of Science* 17: 443–63.

McKinlay, A. and Potter, J. (1987b) 'Social representations: a conceptual critique', *Journal for the Theory of Social Behaviour* 17 (4): 471–87.

McKinlay, A., Potter, J. and Wetherell, M. (1990) 'Discourse analysis and social representations', in G. Breakwell and D. Canter (eds) *Empirical Approaches to Social Representations*, Oxford: Oxford University Press.

Macmillan, A. (1989) 'Developmental narratives: the construction of life stories in therapy', *BPS Psychotherapy Section Newsletter* 7: 19–27.

Mair, M. (1989) 'Psychology as a discipline of discourse', *BPS Psychotherapy Section Newsletter* 7: 2–12.

Mama, A. (1987) 'Race and subjectivity: a study of black women', unpublished Ph.D. thesis, University of London.

Mama, A. (forthcoming) *Beyond the Masks: Race, Gender and the Subject*, London: Routledge.

Manicas, P.T. and Secord, P.F. (1983) 'Implications for psychology of the new philosophy of science', *American Psychologist* 38: 399–413.

Marin, L. (1983) 'Discourse of power – power of discourse: Pascalian notes', in A. Montefiore (ed.) *Philosophy in France Today*, Cambridge: Cambridge University Press.

Marková, I. (1982) *Paradigms, Thought, and Language*, Chichester: Wiley.

Marks, D. (1990) 'Dilemmas of confronting your "subjects": two years after a discourse analysis project', paper given at BPS Social Section conference, Leeds, September.

Marshall, H. and Wetherell, M. (1989) 'Talking about career and gender identities: a discourse analysis perspective', in S. Skevington and D. Baker (eds) *The Social Identity of Women*, London: Sage.

Marshall, H. (1991) 'The Social Construction of Motherhood: An Analysis of Childcare and Parenting Manuals', in E. Lloyd, A. Phoenix and A. Woolett (eds) *Motherhood: Meanings, practices and ideologies*, London: Sage.

Marshall, H. (forthcoming) 'Talking About Good Maternity Care: A Discourse Analysis of the Accounts of Midwives and Health Visitors', in P. Nicholson and J. Ussher (eds) *The Psychology of Women's Health and Health Care*, London: Macmillan.

Marx, K. and Engels, F. (1848/1965) *Manifesto of the Communist Party*, Peking: Foreign Languages Press.

Miall, D.S. (1990) 'Changing the self: the affective plot in literary narratives', *BPS Psychotherapy Section Newsletter* 8: 30–9.

Michael, M. (1986) 'Ordinary explanations as discourse: a critical analysis', unpublished Ph.D. thesis, University of Durham.

Michael, M. (1989) 'Attribution and ordinary explanation: cognitivist predilections and pragmatist alternatives', *New Ideas in Psychology* 7 (3): 231–43.

Michael, M. (1990) 'Intergroup theory and deconstruction', in I. Parker and J. Shotter (eds) *Deconstructing Social Psychology*, London and New York: Routledge.

Michael, M. (forthcoming) 'Knowing Ignorance and Ignoring Knowledge: Discourses of ignorance in the public understanding of science and technology', in A. Irwin and B. Wynne (eds) *Science, Technology and Everyday Life*.

Michael, M. and Still, A. (forthcoming) 'A resource for resistance: J.J. Gibson's notion of "affordance" and power-knowledge', *New Ideas in Psychology*.

Middleton, D. and Edwards, D. (eds) (1990) *Collective Remembering*, London and New York: Sage.

Mills, S. (1990) 'Discourses of difference', *Cultural Studies* 4 (2): 128–40.

Moir, J. (1990) 'Psychological theories and lay accounts of occupational choice: a comparative study of mechanical engineering and nursing undergraduates', unpublished Ph.D. thesis, Dundee Institute of Technology.

Montag, W. (1988) 'What is at stake in the debate on postmodernism?', in E.A. Kaplan (ed.) *Postmodernism and Its Discontents: Theories, Practices*, London: Verso.

Moore, C. (1989) *Divisive Language*, Cambridge: Church in Danger.

Mostyn, B, (1985) 'The content analysis of qualitative research data: a dynamic approach', in M. Brenner, J. Brown and D. Canter (eds) *The Research Interview: Uses and Approaches*, London: Academic Press.

Mudge, L.S. (1987) 'Thinking in the community of faith: toward an ecclesial hermeneutic', in L.A. Mudge and J.N. Poling (eds) *Formation and Reflection: The Promise of Practical Theology*, Philadelphia: Fortress Press.

Mulkay, M. (1985) *The Word and the World: Explorations in the Form of Sociological Analysis*, London: Allen & Unwin.

Mulkay, M., Potter, J. and Yearley, S. (1983) 'Why an analysis of scientific discourse is needed', in K. Knorr-Cetina and M. Mulkay (eds) *Science Observed: Perspectives on the Social Study of Science*, London: Sage.

Murphy, J.W. (1988) 'Making sense of postmodern sociology', *British Journal of Sociology* 39 (4): 600–14.

Noble, W. (1987) 'Perception and language: towards a complete ecological psychology', in A. Costall and A. Still (eds) *Cognitive Psychology in Question*, Hassocks, Sussex: Harvester.

Oakley, A. (1981) 'Interviewing women: a contradiction in terms', in H. Roberts (ed.) *Doing Feminist Research*, London: Routledge & Kegan Paul.

Outhwaite, W. (1987) *New Philosophies of Social Science: Realism, Hermeneutics and Critical Theory*, New York: St. Martins.

Owens, C. (1985) 'The discourse of others: feminists and postmodernism', in H. Foster (ed.) *Postmodern Culture*, London: Pluto Press.

Parker, I. (1987a) ' "Social representations": social psychology's (mis)use of sociology', *Journal for the Theory of Social Behaviour* 17 (4): 447–69.

Parker, I. (1987b) 'The social status of mentalistic constructs', in W.J. Baker, M.E. Hyland, H. van Rappard and A.W. Staats (eds) *Current Issues in Theoretical Psychology*, Amsterdam: North Holland.

Parker, I. (1988a) 'Deconstructing accounts', in C. Antaki (ed.) *Analysing Everyday Explanation: A Casebook of Methods*, London: Sage.

Parker, I. (1988b) 'Abstracts and brief chronicles of the time: review of A. Costall and A. Still (1987)', *BPS History and Philosophy Section Newsletter* 6: 8–10.

Parker, I. (1989a) *The Crisis in Modern Social Psychology, and How to End It*, London: Routledge.

Parker, I. (1989b) 'Discourse and power', in J. Shotter and K.J. Gergen (eds) *Texts of Identity*, London: Sage.

Parker, I. (1989c) 'Research futures: opportunism and AIDS', *BPS Social Psychology Section Newsletter* 21: 7–9.

Parker, I. (1990a) 'Discourse: definitions and contradictions', *Philosophical Psychology* 3 (2): 189–204.

Parker, I. (1990b) 'Real things: discourse, context and practice', *Philosophical Psychology* 3 (2): 227–33.

Parker, I. (1990c) 'The abstraction and representation of social psychology', in I. Parker and J. Shotter (eds) *Deconstructing Social Psychology*, London: Routledge.

Parker, I. (1991a) 'The Manchester Workshop, July 9–11, 1990', *DARG Newsletter*.

Parker, I. (1991b) 'Discourse discourse: social psychology and postmodernity', in J. Doherty, E. Graham and M. Malek (eds) *Postmodernism and the Social Sciences*, London: Macmillan.

Parker, I. (in press) 'Everyday behavior(ism) and therapeutic practice: The ego as verbal nucleus in Skinner and Lacan', in J. Siegfried (ed.) *Therapeutic and Everyday Discourse and Behavior Change: Towards a micro-analysis in psychotherapy process research*, New York: Ablex.

Parker, I. (forthcoming) 'Discourse, reflection and direct perception', *New Ideas in Psychology*.

Parker, I. and Shotter, J. (eds) (1990) *Deconstructing Social Psychology*, London: Routledge.

Peacock, T.L. (1818/1903) *Melincourt*, in *The Novels of Thomas Love Peacock*, London: Simpkin, Marshall, Hamilton, Kent & Co. Ltd.

Pilgrim, D. (1990) 'Researching psychotherapy in Britain: the limits of a psychological approach', in I. Parker and J. Shotter (eds) *Deconstructing Social Psychology*, London: Routledge.

Porpora, D.V. (1989) 'Four concepts of social structure', *Journal for the Theory of Social Behaviour* 19 (2): 195–211.

Potter, J. (1981) 'The development of social psychology: consensus, theory and methodology in the *British Journal of Social Psychology*', *British Journal of Social Psychology* 20: 249–58.

Potter, J. (1983) 'Speaking and writing science: issues in the analysis of psychologists' discourse', unpublished D.Phil. thesis, University of York.

Potter, J. (1985) 'Testability, flexibility: Kuhnian values in scientists' discourse concerning theory choice', *Philosophy of the Social Sciences* 14: 303–30.

Potter, J. (1987) 'Reading repertoires: a preliminary study of some techniques that scientists use to construct readings', *Science and Technology Studies* 15 (3/4): 112–21.

Potter, J. (1988a) 'What is reflexive about discourse analysis? – The case of reading readings', in S. Woolgar (ed.) *Knowledge and Reflexivity: New Frontiers in the Sociology of Knowledge,* London: Sage.

Potter, J. (1988b) 'Cutting cakes: a study of psychologists' social categorizations', *Philosophical Psychology* 1: 17–33.

Potter, J. (1989) 'Loughborough University of Technology, Department of Social Science: research interests and activities', *BPS Social Psychology Section Newsletter* 22: 27–8.

Potter, J. (1990) 'The Loughborough Workshop, March 29–April 1, 1990', *DARG Newsletter* 6 (2): 10–11.

Potter, J. and Collie, F. (1989) ' "Community care" as persuasive rhetoric: a study of discourse', *Disability, Handicap and Society* 4: 57–64.

Potter, J. and Edwards, D. (1990) 'Nigel Lawson's tent: discourse analysis, attribution theory and the social psychology of fact', *European Journal of Social Psychology* 20: 405–24.

Potter, J. and Halliday, Q. (1990) 'Community leaders: a device for warranting versions of crowd events', *Journal of Pragmatics* 14: 225–41.

Potter, J. and Litton, I. (1985) 'Some problems underlying the theory of social representations', *British Journal of Social Psychology* 24: 81– 90.

Potter, J. and Mulkay, M. (1982) 'Making theory useful: utility accounting in social psychologists' discourse', *Fundamenta Scientiae* 3/4: 259–78.

Potter, J. and Mulkay, M. (1985) 'Scientists' interview talk: interviews as a technique for revealing participants' interpretative practices', in

M. Brenner, J. Brown and D. Canter (eds) *The Research Interview: Uses and Approaches*, London: Academic Press.

Potter, J. and Reicher, S. (1987) 'Discourses of community and conflict: the organization of social categories in accounts of a "riot" ', *British Journal of Social Psychology* 26: 25–40.

Potter, J. and Stringer, P. (1980) 'Ambiguities of the home: an empirical examination of the ethogenic theory of social competence', University of Kent: paper given at BPS Social Psychology Section conference, Kent, September.

Potter, J., Stringer, P. and Wetherell, M. (1984) *Social Texts and Context: Literature and Social Psychology*, London: Routledge & Kegan Paul.

Potter, J. and Wetherell, M. (1987) *Discourse and Social Psychology: Beyond Attitudes and Behaviour*, London: Sage.

Potter, J. and Wetherell, M. (1988a) 'Accomplishing attitudes: fact and evaluation in racist discourse', *Text* 8: 51–68.

Potter, J. and Wetherell, M. (1988b) 'The politics of hypocrisy: notes on the discrediting of apartheid's opponents', *BPS Social Psychology Section Newsletter* 19: 30–42.

Potter, J. and Wetherell, M. (1989) 'Fragmented ideologies: accounts of educational failure and positive discrimination', *Text* 9: 175–90.

Potter, J., Wetherell, M., Gill, R. and Edwards, D. (1990) 'Discourse – noun, verb or social practice', *Philosophical Psychology* 3 (2): 205–17.

Poulantzas, N. (1978) *State, Power, Socialism*, London: New Left Books.

Pringle, R. (1989) 'Bureaucracy, rationality and sexuality: the case of secretaries', in J. Hearn, D.L. Sheppard, P. Tancral-Sheriff and G. Burrell (eds) *The Sexuality of Organization*, London: Sage.

Pringle, R. (1991) *Secretaries' Talk*, London: Verso.

Reason, P. and Rowan, J. (eds) (1981) *Human Inquiry: A Sourcebook of New Paradigm Research*, Chichester: Wiley.

Redhead, S. (1990) *The End-of-the-Century Party: Youth and Pop towards 2000*, Manchester: Manchester University Press.

Reichenbach, H. (1947) *Elements of Symbolic Logic*, London: Macmillan.

Reicher, S. (1988) 'Essay review of *Arguing and Thinking*', *British Journal of Social Psychology* 27: 283–8.

Reicher, S. and Potter, J. (1985) 'Psychological theory as intergroup perspective: a comparative analysis of "scientific" and "lay" accounts of crowd events', *Human Relations* 38: 167–89.

Riach, J. (1989) 'Conceptions of "mental illness" and prescriptions for care: a discourse analytic approach', unpublished B.Sc. project, Manchester Polytechnic.

Richards, B. (1989) *Images of Freud: Cultural Responses to Psychoanalysis*, London: Weidenfeld Dent.

Ricoeur, P. (1971) 'The model of the text: meaningful action considered as a text', *Social Research* 38 (3): 529–62.

Ridgway, J. and Benjamin, M. (1987) *PsiFi: Psychological Theories and Science Fictions*, Leicester: British Psychological Society.

Rorty, R. (1980) *Philosophy and the Mirror of Nature*, Oxford: Basil Blackwell.

Rose, N. (1985) *The Psychological Complex*, London: Routledge & Kegan Paul.

Rose, N. (1989) *Governing the Soul*, London: Routledge.

Rowbotham, S., Segal, L. and Wainwright, H. (1979) *Beyond the Fragments: Feminism and the Making of Socialism*, Newcastle and London: NSC/ICP.

Rustin, M. (1987) 'Psychoanalysis, philosophical realism, and the new sociology of science', *Free Associations* 9: 102–36.

Rustin, M. (1989) 'Post-Kleinian psychoanalysis and the post-modern', *New Left Review* 173: 109–28.

Said, E. (1978) *Orientalism*, London: Routledge & Kegan Paul.

Salmon, P. (1989) 'Old age and story telling', *BPS Psychotherapy Section Newsletter* 7: 44–51.

Sampson, E.E. (1981) 'Cognitive psychology as ideology', *American Psychologist* 36 (7): 730–43.

Sampson, E.E. (1989) 'The deconstruction of the self', in J. Shotter and K.J. Gergen (eds) *Texts of Identity*, London: Sage.

Sarup, M. (1988) *An Introductory Guide to Post-structuralism and Postmodernism*, Hassocks, Sussex: Harvester Wheatsheaf.

Saussure, F. de (1974) *Course in General Linguistics*, London: Fontana.

Seidel, G. (1986a) 'Right-wing discourse', in R. Levitas (ed.) *The Ideology of the New Right*, Cambridge: Polity Press.

Seidel, G. (1986b) *The Holocaust Denial: Anti-Semitism, Racism and the New Right*, Leeds: Beyond the Pale Collective.

Seidel, G. (1990) ' "Thank God I said no to AIDS": on the changing discourse of AIDS in Uganda', *Discourse & Society* 1 (1): 61–84.

Sherrard, C. (1988) 'Rhetorical weapons: Chomsky's attack on Skinner', *Educational Psychology* 8 (3): 197–205.

Sherrard, C. (1991) 'Developing discourse analysis', *Journal of General Psychology*.

Shotter, J. (1975) *Images of Man in Psychological Theory*, London: Methuen.

Shotter, J. (1984) *Accountability and Selfhood*, Oxford: Basil Blackwell.

Shotter, J. (1987) 'Cognitive psychology, "Taylorism", and the manufacture of unemployment', in A. Costall and A. Still (eds) *Cognitive Psychology in Question*, Hassocks, Sussex: Harvester.

Shotter, J. (1987) 'The ephemeral "I": transitory personalities in an era of postmodernism', paper given at APA conference, New York, August–September.

Shotter, J. (1990a) 'Wittgenstein and psychology: on our "hook up" to reality', in A. Phillips-Griffiths (ed.) *The Wittgenstein Centenary Lectures*, Cambridge: Cambridge University Press.

Shotter, J. (1990b) 'The social construction of remembering and forgetting', in D. Middleton and D. Edwards (eds) *Collective Remembering*, London: Sage.

Shotter, J. and Gergen, K.J. (eds) (1989) *Texts of Identity*, London: Sage.

Shotter, J. and Newson, J. (1982) 'An ecological approach to cognitive development: implicate orders, joint action and intentionality', in G. Butterworth and P. Light (eds) *Social Cognition: Studies in the Development of Understanding*, Hassocks, Sussex: Harvester.

Sinason, V. (1989) 'The psycholinguistics of discrimination', in B. Richards (ed.) *Crisis of the Self: Further Essays in Psychoanalysis and Politics*, London: Free Association Books.

Sinha, C. (1988) *Language and Representation: A Socio-Naturalistic Approach to Human Development*, London and New York: Harvester Wheatsheaf.

Slaughter, C. (1989) 'Letter', *Socialist Outlook* 16: 33.

Smith, A.M. (1990) 'A symptomatology of an authoritarian discourse: the parliamentary debates on the prohibition of the promotion of homosexuality', *New Formations* 10: 41–65.

Smith, D.E. (1984) 'Textually mediated social organization', *International Social Science Journal* 99: 59–75.

Smith, D.E. (1978) 'K is mentally ill: the anatomy of a factual account', *Sociology* 12: 23–53.

Soyland, A.J. (1988) 'An analysis of mental health professionals' discourse: the role of the clinical psychologist', unpublished M.A. thesis, University of Adelaide.

Spears, R. (1989) 'Essay review of *Ideological Dilemmas*', *British Journal of Social Psychology* 28: 283–5.

Spender, D. (1981) *Man Made Language*, London: Routledge & Kegan Paul.

Spradley, J.P. (1979) *The Ethnographic Interview*, New York: Holt, Rinehart & Winston.

Squire, C. (1989) *Significant Differences: Feminism in Psychology*, London and New York: Routledge.

Squire, C. (1990a) 'Crisis what crisis? Discourses and narratives of the "social" in social psychology', in I. Parker and J. Shotter (eds) *Deconstructing Social Psychology*, London and New York: Routledge.

Squire, C. (1990b) 'Feminism as anti-psychology', in E. Burman (ed.) *Feminists and Psychological Practice*, London and New York: Sage.

Stanley, L. and Wise, S. (1983) *Breaking Out: Feminist Consciousness and Feminist Research*, London: Routledge & Kegan Paul.

Stern, F.G. (1990) 'Derrida, De Man, despair: reading Derrida on De Man's 1940s essays', *Textual Practice* 4 (1): 22–37.

Still, A. (1979) 'Perception and representation', in N. Bolton (ed.) *Philosophical Problems in Psychology*, London: Methuen.

Sting (1981) 'Spirits in the Material World', in *Ghost in the Machine*: A&M CKM 63730.

Stringer, P. (1990) 'Prefacing social psychology: a textbook example', in I. Parker and J. Shotter (eds) *Deconstructing Social Psychology*, London and New York: Routledge.

Stubbs, M. (1983) *Discourse Analysis: The Sociolinguistic Analysis of Natural Language*, Oxford: Basil Blackwell.

Sylvan, R. (1985a) 'A critique of deep ecology', *Radical Philosophy* 40: 2–12.

Sylvan, R. (1985b) 'A critique of deep ecology: Part II', *Radical Philosophy* 41: 10–22.

Tajfel, H. and Fraser, C. (1978) *Introducing Social Psychology*, Harmondsworth: Penguin.

Tara Arts Group (1989) 'Programme notes for *The Government Inspector ALA AFSUR*'.

Thatcher, M. (1989) quoted in *Socialist Worker*, March 19.

Timms, E. and Segal, N. (eds) (1988) *Freud in Exile: Psychoanalysis and its Vicissitudes*, New Haven and London: Yale University Press.

Timpanaro, S. (1980) *On Materialism*, London: Verso.

Trotsky, L. (1933) 'What is National Socialism?', in Trotsky, L. (1975) *The Struggle Against Fascism in Germany*, Harmondsworth: Pelican.

Turkle, S. (1979) *Psychoanalytic Politics: Jacques Lacan and Freud's French Revolution*, London: Burnett Books.

Turner, B.S. (1987) *Medical Power and Social Knowledge*, London and New York: Sage.

Ullah, P. (1990) 'Rhetoric and ideology in social identification: the case of second generation Irish youths', *Discourse & Society* 1 (2): 167–88.

van Dijk, T.A. (ed.) (1985) *Handbook of Discourse Analysis* (4 Vols), London: Academic Press.

Veblen, T. (1899) *The Theory of the Leisure Class*, New York: The Macmillan Company.

Walkerdine, V. (1981) 'Sex, power and pedagogy', *Screen Education* 38: 14–24. Reprinted in M. Arnot and G. Weiner (eds) (1987) *Gender and the Politics of Schooling*, London: Hutchinson.

Walkerdine, V. (1984) 'Some day my prince will come', in A. McRobbie and M. Nava (eds) *Gender and Generation*, London: Macmillan.

Walkerdine, V. (1986) 'Video replay: families, films and fantasy', in V. Burgin, J. Donald and C. Kaplan (eds) *Formations of Fantasy*, London: Methuen.

Walkerdine, V. (1987) 'No laughing matter: girls' comics and the preparation for adolescent sexuality', in J.M. Broughton (ed.) *Critical Theories of Psychological Development*, New York: Plenum Press.

Walkerdine, V. (1988) *The Mastery of Reason*, London: Routledge.

Walkerdine, V. (1991) *Schoolgirl Fictions*, London: Verso.

Warren, K. (1988) 'The child as a problem or the child with needs: a discourse analysis of a case conference', unpublished B.Sc. project, Manchester Polytechnic.

Wartofsky, M. (1980) 'Visual scenarios: the role of representation in pictures', in M.A. Hagen (ed.) *The Perception of Pictures, Vol II*, London and New York: Academic Press.

WAUDAG (Dillon, G.L., Doyle, A., Eastman, C.M., Silberstein, S. and Toolan, M.) (1989) 'Resisting the public discourse of AIDS', *Textual Practice* 3: 388–96.

WAUDAG (Dillon, G.L., Doyle, A., Eastman, C.M., Silberstein, S. and Toolan, M.) (1990) 'The rhetorical construction of a President', *Discourse & Society* 1 (2): 189–200.

Weedon, C. (1987) *Feminist Practice and Post-structuralist Theory*, Oxford: Basil Blackwell.

Wetherell, M. (1986) 'Linguistic repertoires and literary criticism: new directions for the social psychology of gender', in S. Wilkinson (ed.) *Feminist Social Psychology*, Milton Keynes: Open University Press.

Wetherell, M. and Potter, J. (1986) 'Discourse analysis and the social psychology of racism', *BPS Social Psychology Section Newsletter* 15: 24–9.

Wetherell, M. and Potter, J. (1988) 'Discourse analysis and the identification of interpretative repertoires', in C. Antaki (ed.) *Analysing Everyday Explanation: A Casebook of Methods*, London: Sage.

Wetherell, M. and Potter, J. (1989) 'Narrative characters and accounting for violence', in J. Shotter and K.J. Gergen (eds) *Texts of Identity*, London: Sage.

Wetherell, M. and Potter, J. (forthcoming) *Mapping the Language of Racism: Discourse and the Legitimation of Exploitation*, Hassocks, Sussex: Harvester Wheatsheaf.

Wetherell, M., Potter, J. and Stringer, P. (1983) 'Psychology, literature and texts', *Bulletin of the British Psychological Society* 36: 377–9.

Wetherell, M., Stiven, H. and Potter, J. (1987) 'Unequal egalitarianism: a preliminary study of discourses concerning gender and employment opportunities', *British Journal of Social Psychology* 26: 59–71.

White, M. and Epston, D. (1989) *Literate Means to Therapeutic Ends*, Adelaide: Dulwich Centre Publications.

White, S. and Wetherell, M. (1988) 'Fear of fat: a study of discourses concerning eating patterns and body shape', unpublished ms., University of St. Andrews.

Widdicombe, S. (1990) '"Do not ask me who I am and do not ask me to remain the same": Essay review of *Subjectivity and Method in Psychology: Gender, Meaning and Science*', unpublished ms., University of Edinburgh.

Widdicombe, S. and Wooffitt, R. (1990) '"Being" versus "Doing" punk: on achieving authenticity as a member', *Journal of Language and Social Psychology* 9 (3): 1–21.

Williams, R. (1976) *Keywords: A Vocabulary of Culture and Society*, London: Fontana.

Williamson, J. (1986) *Consuming Passions: The Dynamics of Popular Culture*, London: Marion Boyars.

Wooffitt, R. (1988) '(Telling) tales of the unexpected: a sociological analysis of accounts of the paranormal', unpublished D.Phil. thesis, University of York.

Wooffitt, R. and Widdicombe, S. (1990) '"Well what do you expect looking like that": A study of the use of "Ordinary Identity" in the Construction of a Complaint', unpublished ms., University of Surrey.

Woolgar, S. (1988a) *Science: The Very Idea*, London: Ellis Horwood/Tavistock.

Woolgar, S. (1988b) *Knowledge and Reflexivity: New Frontiers in the Sociology of Knowledge*, London and New York: Sage.

Worsthorne, P. (1984) 'Naff remarks by Peregrine Worsthorne', in K. Bryson, S. Fitzherbert and J.-L. Legris (1984) *The Complete Naff Guide*, London: Arrow Books.

Name index

Subject index